Great World Religions: Christianity

Luke Timothy Johnson, Ph.D.

THE
GREAT
COURSES

PUBLISHED BY:

THE GREAT COURSES
Corporate Headquarters
4840 Westfields Boulevard, Suite 500
Chantilly, Virginia 20151-2299
Phone: 1-800-832-2412
Fax: 703-378-3819
www.thegreatcourses.com

Luke Timothy Johnson, Ph.D.
Professor of New Testament
and Christian Origins
Emory University

Professor Luke Timothy Johnson is the Robert W. Woodruff Professor of New Testament and Christian Origins at Candler School of Theology, Emory University, in Atlanta, Georgia. Born in 1943 and from the ages of 19 to 28 a Benedictine monk, Dr. Johnson received a B.A. in Philosophy from Notre Dame Seminary in New Orleans, an M.Div. in Theology from Saint Meinrad School of Theology in Indiana, and an M.A. in Religious Studies from Indiana University, before earning his Ph.D. in New Testament from Yale University in 1976.

Professor Johnson taught at Yale Divinity School from 1976 to 1982 and at Indiana University from 1982 to 1992 before accepting his current position at Emory. He is the author of 20 books, including *The Writings of the New Testament: An Interpretation* (2nd edition, 1998), which is used widely as a textbook in seminaries and colleges. He has also published several hundred articles and reviews. His most recent books are *The Creed: What Christians Believe and Why It Matters* and *The Future of Catholic Biblical Scholarship*. He is working on the influence of Greco-Roman religion on Christianity.

Professor Johnson has taught undergraduates, as well as master's level and doctoral students. At Indiana University, he received the President's Award for Distinguished Teaching, was elected a member of the Faculty Colloquium on Excellence in Teaching, and won the Brown Derby and Student Choice Awards for teaching. At Emory, he has twice received the "On Eagle's Wings Excellence in Teaching" Award. In 1997–1998, he was a Phi Beta Kappa Visiting Scholar, speaking at college campuses across the country.

Professor Johnson is married to Joy Randazzo. They share seven children, 11 grandchildren, and three great-grandchildren. Johnson also teaches the courses called *The Apostle Paul* and *Early Christianity: The Experience of the Divine* for The Teaching Company. ∎

Table of Contents

Table of Contents

SUPPLEMENTAL MATERIAL

Great World Religions: Christianity

Scope:

Christianity is one of religion's great success stories. Beginning as a sect of Judaism in an obscure province of the Roman Empire in the 1st century C.E., it became the official religion of the Roman Empire by the 4th century, dominated the cultural life of Europe for much of its history, and now counts more than two billion adherents throughout the world.

Christianity is also one of the most paradoxical of religions. While bearing a message of peace and unity, it has often been a source of conflict and division. While proclaiming a heavenly kingdom, it has often been deeply involved with human politics. While rejecting worldly wisdom, it has claimed the intellectual allegiance of great minds. These apparent contradictions arise from the complex character of Christianity's claims about God, the world, and above all, Jesus of Nazareth, whose death and resurrection form the heart of the good news proclaimed by this religious tradition.

This course provides a sense of Christianity as a whole in its most essential features. It cannot hope to deal in detail with all the complex variations that have entered into a tradition that has lasted two millennia and extended itself to every nation and virtually every language. The lectures concentrate on the basics. They seek to provide a clear survey of the most important elements of this religious tradition and a framework for the student's further study.

After an opening presentation that situates Christianity among the other world religions, the second and third lectures cover the birth and first expansion of Christianity across the Mediterranean world and its great crisis of self-definition in the middle and late 2nd century. The next five lectures are synthetic in character, providing first an overview of the Christian story (how it understands history from creation to new creation—and the relation of Scripture to that history), the Christian creed (what Christians believe about God, Jesus, the Holy Spirit, and the church), and a sense of Christian practice as expressed, in turn, by the structure of the community and its sacraments, by the struggles of Christians to find a coherent and consistent moral teaching, and by various manifestations of Christianity's more radical edge in martyrs, monks, mendicants, missionaries, and mystics.

The final four lectures deal with internal and external conflicts. The first of these is the division of Christianity into three great families: Orthodox,

Jesus of Nazareth's resurrection from the dead gives birth to this religious movement, and in the further sense Jesus's human story—his words, actions, and manner of death—remain central to Christian identity.

Roman Catholic, and Protestant. The second is the centuries-long struggle to find an appropriate role within the political structures of society. The third is Christianity's past and present engagement with culture and the life of the mind, with particular emphasis on the impact of the Enlightenment. The final lecture takes up the tensions in Christianity today—especially the struggle in the First World between fundamentalism and modernity—and the possibilities for this ancient yet lively religion's future among developing nations.

At the end, students will have a grasp of Christianity's distinctive character, the major turning points in its history, its most important shared beliefs and practices, its sharp internal divisions, its struggles to adapt to changing circumstances, and some sense of its continuing appeal to many of the world's peoples. ∎

Christianity among World Religions
Lecture 1

> A world religion is one whose experience and convictions succeed in organizing a way of life beyond local, ethnic, or national boundaries. ... By any measure, Christianity must be considered one of the world religions.

This class introduces Christianity as a world religion. The obvious first questions to ask are: "What is a religion?" and "What is a world religion?" *Religion* can be defined as "a way of life organized around experiences and convictions concerning ultimate power." The phrase "organized way of life" suggests both the pervasiveness of religious sensibility and the structure of religion, involving specific practices. The phrase "experiences and convictions" points to the way religion responds to and understands the world. The phrase "ultimate power" distinguishes religion from other ways of organizing life.

A world religion is one whose experience and convictions succeed in organizing a way of life beyond local, ethnic, or national boundaries. Some traditions are circumscribed by area, culture, or ethnicity but are considered world religions because of their influence (Hinduism, Judaism). Some traditions have reached beyond local circumstances to encompass many populations and cultures (Buddhism, Islam, Christianity). Some traditions reach the status of world religions, then lose it (Manichaeism).

Christianity claims more adherents than any other religion and is the dominant tradition among many diverse populations. It has 2,000 years of history, making it younger than Judaism, Hinduism, and Buddhism, but older than Islam. It is complex both in terms of its internal development and in terms of its engagement with culture. It is remarkably various in its manifestations, existing not only in three distinct groupings (Orthodox, Roman Catholic, Protestant), but in thousands of specific styles. Most of the world operates on a dating system that revolves around the birth of Jesus: B.C. (before Christ) and A.D. (*anno Domini*).

As a world religion, Christianity's profile is at once distinctive and paradoxical. Christianity has a strong resemblance to other "Western religions," such as Judaism and Islam, yet has distinctive features. All three traditions are monotheistic and view God as creator, revealer, savior, and judge. All are structurally exoteric, yet have strong mystical tendencies. Christianity's claim that Jesus is divine fundamentally alters each of the elements that this tradition shares with Judaism and Islam. Christianity also bears comparison with Buddhism on some important points. Both traditions are grounded in the experience of a specific historical person who becomes the symbolic center around which life is organized. Both traditions have aggressively entered into competition with other religious traditions through practices of proselytism.

More than any other world religion, Christianity is marked by paradox both in its fundamental claims and in its historical manifestations.

More than any other world religion, Christianity is marked by paradox both in its fundamental claims and in its historical manifestations. The "Christ" in Christianity is remarkable for the disparity between his historical life and the significance of his death (and resurrection). Christianity has constantly experienced the tension between proclaimed ideals and lived realities.

An introduction to Christianity makes use of certain basic terms that apply to other traditions as well but have specific meaning in Christianity. The *founder* is the figure regarded by the tradition either as channel or agent of revelation and, often, as the organizer of the way of life. The *community* refers to the members of the way of life and to the forms of organization they may observe. *Scripture* or *sacred texts* are those writings that are regarded as normative for the experiences and convictions of the religious tradition. *Myth* does not mean falsehood but, rather, a story that tries to communicate truths that history cannot. Often, myths have to do with how God is at work among humans. *Doctrine* means the organized and normative form of teaching that guides the religious way of life. *Ritual* refers to those practices by which religions demarcate *sacred time* and *sacred space* through repetitive communal (and often individual) activities (see also *liturgy*). *Morality* is the code of behavior that is considered to follow from the religious experiences and convictions of adherents. *Mysticism* refers specifically to the means by which direct experience of ultimate power is sought within a tradition or, more widely, to practices of prayer and meditation.

This class provides a survey of the most important elements in Christianity and a framework for students' further study. The first two lectures deal with Christianity's birth and expansion across the Mediterranean world in the 1st century of the common era and its crisis of self-definition in the late 2nd century. The following lectures are synthetic, providing an overview of the Christian story, creed, community and worship, moral teaching, and mysticism. The final four lectures address internal and external conflicts: the division into three rival versions, the struggle with politics, the engagement with culture, and tensions within Christianity today. ∎

Supplemental Reading

P. Johnson, *A History of Christianity* (New York: Atheneum, 1976).

M. J. Weaver, *Introduction to Christianity*, 3rd edition, with D. Bakke and J. Bivins (Belmont, CA: Wadsworth Press, 1998).

Questions to Consider

1. Why does the classification "world religion" involve more than the number of adherents claimed by a tradition?

2. Compare Christianity and Buddhism in terms of their respective founders and ideas of salvation.

Christianity among World Religions
Lecture 1—Transcript

Christianity may seem to be so much among us that it scarcely needs introduction. It is among us in many bewildering, different, and often competing ways, however. This means that many, even its adherents, do not know the basic structure of this religion or its history. They also may not understand why it now appears in so many diverse forms.

Many, even its adherents, have never compared Christianity to the other great religions practiced by the majority of the world's populace. They therefore miss Christianity's distinctiveness among the world's other religions. Thus, even for adherents, an introduction to Christianity by way of comparison truly is an introduction.

This approach allows insiders to access Christianity from the outside. It allows outsiders to get some sense of what's inside Christianity. It therefore allows them to discover what's unique and possibly interesting about this religious tradition.

This first class session introduces Christianity as a world religion. The obvious first questions to ask are: What is a religion? What makes a world religion?

Let me begin with a preliminary definition of "religion." *Religion* is "a way of life organized around certain experiences and convictions having to do with ultimate power."

Let me break down that definition a little bit. Religion is first of all an "organized way of life." It is a way of life. Religious people do not think of religion as some segmented part of their existence, but as pervasive for all of their lives. It is not a matter simply of worshipping one hour a week, but of viewing all of reality from a different perspective, and acting because they have that perspective. Thus, it is a way of life, but it is also organized.

Religion is not simply something that happens in the head or in the feelings or in individuals. It is a matter of bodies and of communities. It is a matter of what bodies do, and what communities do together in shared practices. Therefore, it is an organized way of life that involves certain "experiences and convictions."

The religious experiences give birth to religions and to what those religions try to communicate. Joachim Wach, the former sociologist of religion at the University of Chicago, has given a marvelous definition of religious experience. He has said that religious experience is a response to what is perceived as ultimate; it involves the whole person, is characterized by a peculiar intensity, and issues forth an appropriate action.

Religious people do not think that they are making this up. They think that they are responding to something that is ultimately real; because they are responding to this ultimately real thing, they must also respond and organize their lives in a certain fashion.

The practice of religion also involves more than experiences. It involves convictions. Religions construct the world in a certain way. They interpret reality in a certain way. Their adherents, who share similar experiences and convictions, really do have a different world than those who do not share those experiences and convictions.

Finally, the phrase "ultimate power" is important. People who are religious think that they are not organizing their life around the pursuit of money, the pursuit of pleasure, or the pursuit of political power. Rather, they are responding to that which goes beyond the human manipulation of power. They are responding to something that is transcendent and goes beyond the pleasurable, the beautiful, the useful, and even the good. They are responding to that which is, in some sense, ultimate.

Religion, then, is a way of life organized around the experience of ultimate power, and is characterized by certain experiences and convictions. If that's our definition of religion, then what makes a religion a world religion?

A world religion is one whose experiences and convictions succeed in organizing life beyond local, ethnic, national, or cultural boundaries. A tribal religion, let us say an African tribal religion, or a North American tribal religion, is totally complete as a religion. It totally interprets the world. It is perfectly satisfactory as a way of organizing existence, but it is so only for a single tribe, only for a very localized region.

A world religion is one that goes beyond those boundaries. It is true that some traditions are circumscribed by area, culture, or ethnicity, but are nevertheless considered world religions because of their influence.

The outstanding example of this among Eastern religions is Hinduism. There are some 813 million Hindus in Asia. By the way, I'm taking all of my figures that I share with you in this first presentation from the 2003 edition of the World Almanac. It reports information on the self-reported adherence of these various traditions. There are 813 million Hindus in Asia, but there are no more than two million Hindus in any other part of the globe. Nevertheless, Hinduism is regarded as a world religion because it gave birth to Buddhism, which is a world-encompassing religious tradition.

Even more striking, of course, is Judaism. There are only 14.5 million Jews in the world today, and they are very much ethnic in character. Jews consider themselves to be an extended family, the children of Abraham. Yet Judaism has given rise to two of the most populous world religions, Christianity and Islam. Because of this influence, Judaism is regarded as a world religion. Some other traditions have manifestly extended themselves beyond local circumstances to encompass many populations and cultures. In the East, Buddhism is the great example of this.

Buddhism began in India, and has spread throughout Asia and the world. There are 350 million Buddhists in Asia today, but there are 1.5 million Buddhists in Europe and 2.7 million Buddhists in North America.

Islam is an even more outstanding example among Western traditions. Beginning among tribes in Saudi Arabia, it has extended itself to every part of the inhabited world, and now counts 1.2 billion adherents worldwide.

There are even some traditions that once had the status of world religions, but don't any longer. The outstanding example of this is Manicheism. Beginning in Persia in the fourth century, it extended itself across virtually every inhabited part of the world, including North Africa, Europe, Central Asia, and East Asia. For a period of some six centuries, it encompassed more than eight different language groups. It was truly a world religion, but disappeared. It's very, very difficult to find somebody claiming to be a Manicheist these days. Thus, world religions can cease being world religions if they lose that capacity to extend themselves across cultures.

By any measure, Christianity must be considered one of the world religions. It claims more adherents than any other religion. There are two billion people on the earth today that claim to be Christian. It is the dominant religious tradition among many diverse populations.

It is striking to realize that there are more Christians in Africa than there are Muslims today. There are some 368 million Christians in Africa, and 323 million Muslims.

There are 559 million Christians in Europe. The next-largest group are those who are simply non-adherents of any religious tradition. There are 486 million Christians in South America. The next largest group of religions is the Spiritists; these are native religionists, numbering about 12 million. There are 261 million Christians in North America. Again, the next largest group is 28 million people who claim to be non-adherents of any religious tradition. In Oceana, there are 25 million Christians, compared to only 367,000 Muslims and 307,000 Buddhists.

Firstly, Christianity's reach is astonishingly large and world-encompassing in terms of adherents.

Secondly, it is ancient. It has 2,000 years of history, and has organized a lot of people's lives for a very long time. It is, to be sure, younger than Hinduism, Buddhism, and Judaism, but it is considerably older than Islam, which has a history of about 1,300 years.

Thirdly, Christianity is complex, both in its internal development and in its cultural engagements.

Now, I will be spending a great deal of this class talking about Christianity's internal developments and the complexities thereof. It is nonetheless important to recognize that Christianity has engaged and been transformed by—and transformed in turn—Jewish culture, Greco-Roman culture, European culture, Asian culture, African culture, and the cultures of South and North America.

Fourthly, it is remarkably diverse in its manifestations. It exists in three major families: the Eastern Orthodox, the Roman Catholic, and the Protestant versions of Christianity. We'll talk about that in a later lecture. The Protestant version itself is subdivided into hundreds of different groups.

It also exists in many different lifestyles. Christians have been martyrs, they've been monks, they've been mendicants, they've been missionaries, and they've been mystics.

They live alone as hermits, out of conviction. They live together in communities and in communes. They worship in basilicas or in cathedrals. Some of them worship at drive-in movies. Some of them worship, they say, through TV broadcasts. They include the most highly intellectual sorts of people: scientists, philosophers, theologians, and they are the most ignorant and benighted of folks. They include the most wealthy and powerful of the European populations, and the most miserably poor of Rio de Janeiro.

Fifthly, Christianity's influence can perhaps most simply be stated by the fact that most of the world operates on a dating system that revolves around the birth of Jesus. The letters "B.C." mean "before Christ." "A.D." in Latin is *anno Domini*, or the "year of the Lord." Even though most of us, especially scholars, have now shifted to the more neutral designations that I will use: "Before the Common Era" is "B.C.E.;" and "C.E.," the "Common Era," it still remains true that the point of pivot is in fact the birth of Jesus Christ.

For all of these reasons: Its size, its history, its complexity and cultural engagement, the variety of its manifestations, and the fact that it organizes the time of much of the world's calendar, Christianity is a true world religion.

Now, as a world religion, Christianity is at once distinctive and paradoxical. Christianity has strong family resemblances to the other so-called Western religions of Judaism and Islam. All three are monotheistic traditions. Judaism, Christianity, and Islam all claim that there is but a single ultimate power that has created all of reality; it has revealed itself to humans and gives them commandments. It is the savior of humans, and is the judge of humans. All three of these traditions are structurally exoteric; that is, they are public and communal traditions in which humans perceive themselves as obligated to observe a certain way of life, in order to please that one God through observance of that God's commandments. This is open and public.

At the same time, all three traditions have very strong mystical tendencies. In Judaism, there is the tradition of Cabalism. In Islam, there is the Sufi tradition. And in Christianity, there are mystics running from the Gnostics of the second century all the way to the Quakers of the 20th century.

Despite these family resemblances with Judaism and Islam, however, Christianity emerges as distinctive above all because of its claim that Jesus of Nazareth is divine. This changes everything. Jesus partakes in creation, revelation, and the saving and judging of humans. He will judge the living and the dead.

By making one who was a human person divine, Christianity's monotheism is obviously quite much more complex than that of Islam and Judaism. Indeed, Judaism, from the beginning, considered Christians to be polytheists. They claim that Christians made two powers in heaven, and therefore are no longer Jewish.

Likewise, the Qur'an speaks of Christians as having given a partner to Allah because they have made Jesus divine. Therefore, they also have shirked, that is, they have fallen back, into idolatry and polytheism.

Christians, of course, claim that they are thoroughly monotheistic, but they think of God's oneness not in terms of singularity but in terms of unity, a unity of divine persons.

Christianity also has striking resemblances with Buddhism on some important points. Both Buddhism and Christianity begin in the experience of a specific historical person. In the case of Buddhism, this is Prince Siddhartha. In the case of Christianity, this is Jesus. The experience of this individual historical person makes that person subsequently the symbol, the Buddha, the Christ, around which adherents organize.

Both traditions as well are aggressively competitive with other traditions. Buddhism, beginning in India, tried to convert others. It entered into competition with Hinduism, with native Chinese religions, and with Taoism; it brought people into the organization of Buddhism through conversion. In a very strikingly similar fashion, Christianity did this with Jews and Greco-Roman culture.

More than any other world religion, however, Christianity is marked by paradox, both in its fundamental claims and in its historical manifestations. The Christ in Christianity is remarkable for the disparity between the historical life of Jesus and the claims that Christians make about Jesus. Here we have a figure who worked for—at most—one to three years in public, gathered a very small band of followers, and was executed under Roman authority as a criminal. His was not a successful career.

Yet because of convictions concerning what happened to Jesus after his death, that is, his resurrection, Christians claim of him that he is cosmic Lord, that he shares the very life of God. Indeed, they claim that Jesus is God incarnate, God in flesh, and in humanity. This gap between who Jesus was historically and what Christians claim of him, and Christianity's capacity to make that claim plausible to millions of people throughout the world, is a deep puzzle to those who do not share in that experience and conviction.

Christianity is paradoxical in another sense, however. It has constantly experienced the tension between the ideals that it proclaims and the actual ways in which it is lived. There is no religious tradition, for example, that gives more value to the idea of unity. Yet Christianity has experienced dissension and division from within from the beginning; now, as I have mentioned, it exists in countless forms that are often competing rivals.

There is no tradition for which peace is a more important idea. Jesus is called the "Prince of Peace." Yet Christianity all too often has aligned itself with warlike tendencies, and has itself caused violence to be done. Christianity likes to think of itself as catholic, that is, as universal, and as embracing all humanity. Yet, in its actually lived manifestations, Christianity has far too often been sectarian, narrow, and parochial.

Christianity thinks of itself as having the ideal of holiness, that is, of representing in the world something of God's own life. Yet in actual fact, Christianity has often been proven to be corrupt, both in power and in possessions.

Now, as we turn to this introduction to Christianity, I want to introduce certain basic terms that are used in all religions, but have a specific meaning in the study of Christianity.

The first is the term *founder*. We use the term *founder* for the one who in the tradition is either the channel or the agent of revelation, and is often the organizer of the way of life. As we shall see in our very next presentation, Jesus is a very problematic founder of Christianity.

The second term is *community*. This is the body of people whose lives are organized around the experiences or the revelations of the founder. In Christianity, the term used for this community is church. The word "church," in Greek *ekklesia*, means first of all not a building, but a gathering. It is an assembly of people. The community is the group that is gathered by this experience.

The third term is *scripture*, or *sacred texts*. Not all religious traditions have sacred texts. Some are quite content to be without scriptures. Some have scriptures, but they're quite diffuse. Nobody knows where Taoist scriptures begin or end; they go on forever.

Christianity, however, has a very restricted set of sacred texts. They are the same as those read by Jews in their Tanakh. The Tanakh is namely the Hebrew Bible, and is called the Old Testament by Christians. There are also 27 writings composed in the first generation of the Christian movement called the New Testament.

The fourth term is *myth*. As used by students of religion, *myth* does not mean falsehood as opposed to history, nor does it mean fiction. Rather, it is used to describe a story that tries to communicate truths that history cannot communicate. Often, myths have to do with the story of how God is at work among humans. In Christianity, this myth, as we will show in a succeeding lecture, is extraordinarily complex.

The fifth term is *doctrine*. The word means teaching. It is the organized and normative form of teaching that guides people in their religions. Again, many religions don't have a great deal of doctrine. Christianity has an extraordinary complex form of doctrine, however. This is because belief, "right thinking," "right belief"—called "orthodoxy" and derived from the Greek word "*opinion*"—has always been very important. We'll devote a whole lecture to what is meant by "right teaching" within Christianity. It is formulated in the creed. The word *creed* comes from the Latin word "*credo*," "*I believe*." The creed is the formulation of Christian doctrine to which all Christians subscribe.

The sixth term is *ritual*. As used by religionists, the term *ritual* refers to the repeated communal actions—communal even when they're done by individuals, which help demarcate *sacred time* and *sacred space*. Sacred time and sacred space are the places of power within a tradition.

The word "ritual" can also be called "worship" or *liturgy*. In Christianity, as we will see, the main forms of ritual are baptism, the ritual of initiation, and the Lord's Supper, or the Eucharist, which is a common meal.

Depending on which version of Christianity one subscribes to, there are many other rituals. In Roman Catholicism, for example, rituals are endless and include any number of individual and communal practices.

The seventh term is *morality*. This is the code of behavior that is thought to follow from the religious experiences and convictions of adherents. Remember Joachim Wach's definition. This religious experience issues in appropriate action. One appropriate action is to organize sacred time and sacred space: "Let's gather around this power."

Another appropriate action is behavior. How do we act in the rest of our lives because of these experiences and convictions? In some traditions, morality is very straightforward, and can be codified in the form of law. This is the case in Islam and Judaism. Morality is not a highly problematic issue. In Christianity, moral teaching is one of the most complex and disputed aspects of this tradition. We will devote an entire lecture to trying to sort that out.

The eighth term is *mysticism*. *Mysticism* refers specifically to the means by which adherents of a religion seek a direct experience of the divine, and, more broadly, to the practices of prayer and meditation by which that direct access may be achieved.

Notice that doctrine, morality, community, and ritual are all mediations. All of these are structures through which the power of religious experience can be channeled to adherents. Mysticism is fascinating because it is the attempt through prayer or through meditation, to bypass those means of mediation. Mysticism is always individual in character, rather than group in character. It always seeks direct access to ultimate power, rather than mediated access to ultimate power. Therefore, it is an extraordinarily enlivening feature of religions, but it also can be, as we shall see, subversive within religious traditions.

In this class, I want to provide a survey of the most important elements of Christianity, and a framework for your future study. First, I want to emphasize Christianity as a religion. It is this aspect of Christianity that so often is missed because Christianity is so deeply involved in politics, in culture, and so forth. I want to give people some sense of how Christianity has been—and continues to be—a powerfully attractive way of life around which people want to organize their own existences.

At the same time, however, I want to give some sense of this complexity, and some sense of the ways in which that religious essence is camouflaged by Christianity's involvement in politics and in culture.

Thus, our first two lectures following this one will deal with Christianity's birth and its expansion across the Mediterranean world in the first century, and then the crisis of self-definition that happened in the second century. I will argue that Christianity really becomes Christianity not in the first century, but in the second century.

The following lectures, then, are synthetic in character. They will provide an overview of the Christian thing. What is the story that Christians tell themselves? What is their creed? What is it that they believe? How do they structure their community and their ritual? What are their moral teachings? What forms of radical observance, including mysticism, do we find among Christians?

In the final four lectures, we want to address the internal and external conflicts that Christians have experienced. Those four synthetic lectures, by and large, provide the ideal. The last four lectures will get down to, first, Christianity's division into three great families. How did that come about?

Then we'll talk about Christianity's involvement in politics, and then its involvement in culture. Finally, we'll discuss the tensions within Christianity today in the First World; we'll also discuss the exciting possibilities for Christianity today, especially in the Third World. This will be, I think, an interesting and exciting course, and I'm glad to be with you in it.

Birth and Expansion
Lecture 2

How did a small sect within 1st-century Judaism become a world religion?

Jesus of Nazareth both is and is not the founder of Christianity. He is not the founder of the religion in the sense that Muhammad is the founder of Islam or even in the sense that Prince Siddharta is the founder of Buddhism: Christianity begins after Jesus's death. Yet Jesus is more than a purely symbolic figure. He is the "founder" of Christianity in the sense that his resurrection from the dead gives birth to a religious movement and in the sense that his human story remains central to Christian identity.

The historical activity of Jesus is difficult to reconstruct with precision but is best understood as a form of prophetic activity within Judaism that is marked by particular urgency and authority and whose proclamation of God's rule issues in a nascent community. The difficulties of historical reconstruction are attributable to the fact that, apart from a few outsider reports, we are dependent on insider Christian writings, above all, the Gospels of Matthew, Mark, Luke, and John, whose narratives depend on an earlier oral tradition and are told from the perspective of faith in Jesus as the Son of God.

Despite these difficulties, we can state definite things about the historical Jesus. His characteristic speech and action identify him as a prophetic figure in the symbolic world of Torah. His proclamation of the rule of God and call to repentance has a special sense of urgency and a special appeal to the outcast. Although the designations *Son of man* and *Christ* are problematic for his lifetime, he speaks and acts with a distinctive sense of authority. His choice of 12 followers symbolizes the restoration of Israel as God's people. In the context of a deeply divided 1st-century Judaism, Jesus met conflict with Jewish leaders and was executed by crucifixion under Roman authority.

Christianity is born as a religion centered on the revelation of God in Jesus Christ through the resurrection experience. The proper understanding of the Resurrection is critical to grasping Christianity's claims. The claim is not that Jesus was resuscitated and continued his mortal existence but that he transcended mortality by entering into a share in God's life and power. The essential designation of Jesus as "Lord" signifies that Jesus has been exalted to the status of God and has become "Life-Giving Spirit" (1 Cor 15:45). The Resurrection is not historical but eschatological, a "new creation" that transforms humans through a new power of life.

The Resurrection is the basis for other fundamental convictions concerning Jesus. The Resurrection reveals what Jesus was already in his mortal life, namely, God's unique Son. The Resurrection is the premise for the expectation

The Christian movement established communities across the Roman Empire with unparalleled rapidity, and the conditions of its expansion meant that it was diverse from the beginning.

that Jesus will come again as judge of the world. The Resurrection makes Jesus not simply a Jewish messiah (in fact, he fails at that) but establishes him as "a new Adam," the start of a new humanity. The Resurrection is the basis for Christianity becoming a worldwide religion rather than a sect within Judaism.

The Christian movement established communities across the Roman Empire with unparalleled rapidity, and the conditions of its expansion meant that it was diverse from the beginning. In the span of 25 years, churches (*ekklesiai*) had been founded from Jerusalem to Rome. The expansion testifies to the power of religious experience, because it was accompanied by persecution and lacked central controls. From the beginning, Christians managed five critical transitions: geographical, sociological, linguistic, cultural, and demographic. The movement was powerful but diverse. By far the most significant transition was the inclusion of Gentile believers without any requirement of observing Jewish customs.

Our earliest Christian letters testify to the liveliness of the religious spirit in these communities and to their problems as well. Paul's letters (for example, 1 Cor) reveal communities meeting in households, manifesting a variety of "spiritual gifts," and practicing common rituals. They also show the presence of severe disagreements concerning the proper way to translate the powerful experience of the Resurrection into consistent patterns of behavior.

The New Testament is a collection of 27 compositions in Greek that were written before the end of the 1st century in response to the needs of early communities. For the first believers, *Scripture* was the Jewish Bible, and each writing in the New Testament represents a reinterpretation of the Jewish Scripture in light of the experience of a crucified and raised messiah. The New Testament contains 13 letters attributed to Paul (the Apostle to the Gentiles), 2 to Peter, 3 to John, 1 each to James and Jude, and an anonymous sermon addressed "to the Hebrews," as well as a historical narrative concerning the first generation (the Acts of the Apostles) and a visionary composition called the Book of Revelation. These writings concentrate on the life and practice of the church and reveal the complexity and energy of the movement. In them, Jesus appears mainly as the present and powerful Lord, but his human example also plays a role.

The New Testament also contains 4 narratives called Gospels that are attributed (in probably chronological sequence) to Mark, Matthew, Luke, and John. These narratives provide a rich collection of Jesus's sayings and deeds as remembered by a community that now believed in him as Lord of creation. The evangelists tell and retell the story of Jesus in a manner that instructs the church in discipleship. Although they use shared traditions and although Matthew, Mark, and Luke (the synoptic Gospels) are literarily interdependent, the Gospels are remarkable for their diverse portrayals of Jesus. Equally remarkable, although written from the perspective of faith, they render the human Jesus as a 1st-century Jew with remarkable accuracy. ■

Essential Reading

Acts of the Apostles.

Gospel of Luke.

Paul's First Letter to the Corinthians.

Supplemental Reading

Luke T. Johnson, *The Writings of the New Testament: An Interpretation*, 2nd revised edition (Minneapolis: Fortress Press, 1998).

W. A. Meeks, *The First Urban Christians: The Social World of the Apostle Paul* (New Haven: Yale University Press, 1983).

Questions to Consider

1. Consider the complex understanding of Jesus as Christianity's founder, both with regard to his human history and his Resurrection. How can this give rise to a variety of interpretations?

2. Why is the Resurrection of Jesus such a key to the understanding of Christianity, especially as a "world religion"?

Birth and Expansion
Lecture 2—Transcript

In our first lecture, we saw that Christianity is the largest of the world's religions, claiming more adherents in more parts of the globe than any other religious tradition. We also saw that its beginnings were, at the very least, inauspicious. Its founder was a man who was executed as a criminal under Roman authority. The gap between these inauspicious beginnings, and the remarkable success Christianity has had in gaining adherence throughout the centuries and even today, is one of history's most interesting stories.

In this presentation, I want to take up the birth and earliest expansion of Christianity in order to sharpen that problem a bit. Let me begin with the simple statement that Jesus of Nazareth both is, and is not, the founder of Christianity. He is not the founder of Christianity in the sense that Muhammad is the founder of Islam, or that Prince Siddhartha is the founder of Buddhism.

In the case of Muhammad, we have somebody who received revelations from Allah over the course of an entire adult life, had them written in the Qur'an, and, in effect, created a system of life for an entire people—a theocracy that could be codified in law.

Jesus's ministry lasted only from one to three years. He delivered himself of odd and parabolic discourse rather than of a system of law, and he was executed shortly thereafter.

In the case of Siddhartha, we have somebody who achieved nirvana and was able to communicate and engender that same experience among others through the teaching of the Four Noble Truths.

Christians do not think that they have the same experience that Jesus did, but rather that they experience Jesus in a different way. Thus, Jesus is not the founder of Christianity in the sense that those other two great religious founders are of their respective traditions.

Yet, Jesus is certainly more than simply a symbolic figure. He is the founder of Christianity in the sense that his resurrection from the dead gives birth to this religious movement, and in the further sense that Jesus's human story—his words, his actions, and his manner of death—remain central to Christian identity.

Now, the historical activity of Jesus of Nazareth is difficult to reconstruct with precision. It is best understood as a form of prophetic activity within Judaism that is marked by a particular urgency and authority, and whose proclamation of God's rule issues in a nascent community.

Let me take each part of that very long sentence and unpack it. First, let me talk about the difficulties of reconstructing the historical Jesus as he existed in first century Palestine. He really was a historical figure. He really did exist. He was a Jew living in Palestine under the reign of Tiberius Caesar. The difficulties of historical reconstruction have to do with our sources. We have very few outsider accounts of Jesus or of the early Christians. There are a few passing mentions in the works of the Roman historians Tacitus and Suetonius, and a possible paragraph in the voluminous works of the Jewish historian Josephus.

Apart from those slender and largely dismissive remarks, however, we are almost totally dependent upon the Christian writings themselves, the earliest of which are the Letters of Paul. These were written between the years 50 and 65 of the C.E. We also have the Gospels of Matthew, Mark, Luke, and John that can be dated roughly between the years 70 and 90 of the C.E. Those narratives depend upon an earlier oral tradition that occurred over a period of some 40 years, in which the memory of Jesus was handed on in Christian communities.

Furthermore, those gospels are told from the perspective of the Resurrection. In other words, they are not neutral accounts. They are far from eyewitness accounts. They are, rather, religious witnesses and interpretations which seek to communicate the convictions of the Christian community. They are written from the perspective of belief in the fact that Jesus is now the risen Lord, the Resurrected One. In other words, the earliest Christian writings do not give us very good historical sources in order to present a reconstruction of Jesus as a purely historical figure. These difficulties are formidable and are difficult to overcome. That's why the attempts to recover the so-called historical Jesus are so problematic.

Nevertheless, with great care, we are able to say some things about Jesus that are historically highly probable. First, his characteristic speech and action identifies him as a prophetic figure within the symbolic world of Torah. Jesus's speech and actions are best understood as having been those of somebody who thought as a Jew would have thought in that era. He appears in these narratives as a prophetic figure similar to that of Elijah in the Old Testament. He is a wandering figure. He is a wonder-working figure; he is not one who occupies a specific space, as did Muhammad, standing on his stump in the backyard delivering messages from Allah.

Jesus's most distinctive proclamation was of the rule of God, the kingdom of God, and that this rule of God was now imminent. Thus, there's a certain urgency to his proclamation. It bears within it a call to repentance. That's similar to what the other prophets did in Israel; they called people back to a renewed commitment to this God by an internal transformation and a change of behavior.

Therefore, Jesus had a particular urgency: "The time is now." "The time has come to completion." "Repent and believe in the good news."

His proclamation also had a distinctive appeal to the outcasts. He did not address himself to the religious elite among the people, but rather to the outcasts. "Blessed are you poor," rather than "you rich." His ministry was characterized by an open-table fellowship with sinners and tax collectors, people who were outcasts among the Jewish people.

Although the very odd designation *Son of man* may in fact have been used of Jesus about himself, the way we find it used in the Gospels clearly reflects later interpretation in the light of the Book of Daniel; Daniel portrays the Son of Man as a messianic and ruling figure.

The designations *Son of man*, *Christ*, *Messiah*, and *Anointed One* are very problematic of Jesus during his lifetime. In other words, it's not probable that anybody gave him that high status during his lifetime, not even his followers. Nevertheless, Jesus speaks with a distinctive sense of authority. He interprets Torah. He interprets Scripture, the Jewish law—not as other Jewish teachers of that time did by referring to other authorities, but simply on his own authority. "You have heard it said, but I say to you."

In fact, one of his most characteristic locutions is the outrageous prefacing of his remarks by the word "Amen." "Amen, Amen, I say to you." "Amen" is usually something that one says to somebody else in order to assent to what he or she says. In other words, Jesus's sense of authority is communicated by the fact that he self-validates his speech before he even begins it.

Jesus's choice of 12 followers is virtually historically certain, and it indicates that he had some sense of beginning a movement; this movement was understood as somehow the restoration of Israel itself. The 12 followers clearly matched the symbolic figures of the 12 tribes of Israel.

In the context of a deeply divided first-century Judaism, Jews in Palestine in the first century were deeply divided over what the proper response to Greco-Roman culture and Roman rule was. There were many different divisions; there were the Pharisees, Sadducees, Essenes, and zealots—all of whom wanted the kingdom of God, and each whom wanted the rule of God. However, each had very different notions of how these things should come about.

Jesus's own distinctive proclamation of this rule of God inevitably ran into conflict with other Jewish leaders, because it was connected to his own wonder-working and to his own inclusion of outcasts among the people. He finally met his death, and was executed by crucifixion. Crucifixion was the most painful and shameful form of execution; it was fit only for slaves, under the Roman authority of *Pontius Pilate*, and probably happened around the year 30.

Therefore, although provocative and highly fascinating, Jesus's historical ministry came to a screeching halt. His followers disbanded. Indeed, the early Roman observer Tacitus remarks that this movement began in Judea, stopped, and then started up again.

It's that gap between Jesus's failure to convert all his fellow Jews and really begin something, and the rise of Christianity that is the most puzzling feature of this religion. Christianity was born as a religion because of the Resurrection experience. It was not born because of what Jesus said and did during his lifetime, but because of the experience and convictions of his followers after his death.

Therefore, understanding the Resurrection, and what Christians mean by the Resurrection, is critical to grasping Christianity's claim. This is the part of Christianity that is most offensive to Enlightenment reason, and indeed to ancient reason. It says that that an ordinary human person is not only raised from the dead and resuscitated, but now shares God's life. It is, however, the very thing that makes Christianity a powerful and compelling religious movement.

We need to understand what Christians are claiming by the Resurrection. The claim is not that Jesus didn't really die, but that he went to be with God. That, in fact, is the Qur'an's explanation of Jesus's sharing in heaven with Allah.

Nor do Christians claim that Jesus was resuscitated and continued his mortal existence. There are many, many stories—both ancient and modern—about resuscitations. These are about people who experience clinical death, and then recover and go back to their ordinary existence. However, Resuscitation means simply that mortality is not transcended, but simply deferred. People who are resuscitated ultimately die. They continue to be mortal.

What Christians claim of Jesus is that he transcended mortality by entering into a share of God's life and power. Thus, it's not simply that he went back to work on Easter Sunday, but rather that he entered into a full participation of God's life. This is image in terms of an exultation or an enthronement. Psalm

110:1 says, "The Lord said to my Lord, sit at my right hand until I make your enemies a footstool at your feet." This became the way that Christians understood the Resurrection. It is not resuscitation. It is an enthronement, an exultation to share God's life.

The essential and earliest designation of Christians, "Jesus is Lord," as in I Corinthians 12:3, is not acknowledging that Jesus is a powerful human person. It is saying that Jesus shares the life of God. We know this because the word "Lord" in Greek is *Kyrios*. *Kyrios* is used in the Greek translation of the Hebrew Scriptures, called the *Septuagint*, for the distinctive name of Israel's God, Yahweh. This personal name of God, Kyrios, is now applied to Jesus.

Therefore, when the earliest Christians said, "Jesus is Lord," they were, in effect, saying, "Jesus is God." He has been exalted to the status of God and has become, as Paul says in I Corinthians 15:45, "Life-Giving Spirit." Only God can give life, so what Paul is saying is that Jesus did not just regain his life. He became the source of life to others through this energy, the radiation of this energy field that Christians call the Holy Spirit.

Thus, the Resurrection, in this sense, is not an historical event, by definition. Christians would refer to it as an eschatological event, meaning that it denotes the ending of one kind of history and the beginning of another. The closest comparison that Paul can find to this event is creation itself, so he refers to the fact that if anybody is in Christ, there is a new creation. Jesus's Resurrection, then, is seen as the vehicle through which to provide the possibility of transforming all humans through a new power of life. It's a remarkable, powerful, and paradoxical claim, but it is the claim that is the basis for other fundamental convictions concerning Jesus.

Firstly, the Resurrection reveals for Christians what Jesus already was implicitly in his mortal life; namely, he was God's unique Son. This means by around the year 55 or 56, Paul's Letter to the Philippians begins by saying, "Although he was in the form of God, he emptied himself out and took the form of humans." When Jesus was among other humans in mortal form, it was a kind of "emptying out" of the obvious divinity, but he was nevertheless really God among humans.

Secondly, in light of the Resurrection, Christians read back from this experience to Jesus's ministry and ultimately even to his birth. They therefore hold that Jesus is incarnate God. He is God in flesh among humans. The Resurrection experience, furthermore, is the premise for the expectation that Jesus will come again as judge of the living and the dead. This means that God's triumph has begun with Jesus, but it's not complete. Jesus will be the future judge of humans, because in fact he shares God's life and power now as Lord.

Thirdly, the Resurrection makes Jesus not simply a Jewish messiah. Indeed, he's a failed Jewish messiah. I mean, clearly things did not get better for Jews because of Jesus. Indeed, in Jewish eyes, Jesus is not only a failed messiah, but also possibly a false messiah.

For Christians, Jesus is inadequately described as *Christ* or as *Messiah*. He is rather a new Adam, and the start of a new humanity. In some sense, the Resurrection experience is "God's beginning of a new way of being human," as Paul says in Romans 5:12-21, "It is not just for Jews, but for all people."

Finally, it is the Resurrection that makes Christianity potentially a worldwide religion, rather than a sect within Judaism. If Jesus had been a successful messiah within Judaism, Christianity would have remained a sect within Judaism. Christianity's claims are potentially worldwide. Jesus is the start of a new creation, and this is based on the Resurrection.

It is not a matter, then, of political or a temporary rule over a certain population. Rather, it is the possibility of human transformation throughout all time. This is a very powerful kind of experience, and a very powerful claim. On this basis, the Christian movement established communities across the Roman Empire with unparalleled rapidity.

The conditions of its expansion meant that it was diverse from the beginning. Within a span of 25 years, Christians established communities from Jerusalem all the way to Rome. The rapidity of this expansion was unsupported by any political or economic means of significance. This testifies to the power of religious experience. It's also a possible testimony to the unpopularity of Christianity among Jews as it was moved from place to place, not because everybody liked it, but because a lot of people disliked it.

The rapidity of its spread is also impressive, however, because it was accompanied by persecution, and because it did not have real textual or organizational controls. It really seemed to simply move almost spontaneously. From the beginning, Christianity had to accomplish five fundamental transitions, not after a long period of stability, but rather from the get-go. It had to accomplish a geographical transition from Palestine to the Diaspora, to all of the lands outside Palestine.

It was a sociological transition. Jesus was a rural itinerant preacher. The first Christians we meet were urban, living in the big cities in the Roman Empire. The growth of Christianity involved a linguistic transition from Aramaic to Greek. It involved a cultural transition from a predominantly Jewish culture to a predominantly Greco-Roman culture. Finally, it involved a demographic transition; it evolved from being a movement among Jews to an ever-increasing movement among non-Jews or Gentiles.

Thus, this was a powerful movement. The point I want to make is that the very power and rapidity of its spread, its lack of controls, and the transitions that it had to accomplish meant that Christianity was diverse from the beginning. In other words, everywhere Christianity appeared, it was something slightly different. What is remarkable about Christianity is not that it should be diverse, but that it should have any unity at all.

By far the most important of these transitions in that first generation and in that first expansion, was the inclusion of Gentiles into the community without the obligations of circumcision or observance of Jewish law. It doesn't matter whether there was an episodic council in the year 49 or not; as portrayed by Luke in the Acts of the Apostles, this was when church leaders gathered to debate this issue.

It is quite clear that already in the first generation, Gentiles were being allowed into the community not by requiring them to first become Jews, but simply on their own terms. This meant that almost from the beginning, and in the light of the Resurrection, Christianity saw itself as a potential worldwide religion.

Our earliest Christian letters testified to the liveliness of the religious spirit in these communities, and to their problems as well. First Corinthians, which are Paul's letters and are our earliest Christian writings, reveal that there were communities that met in ordinary households. They were drawn from diverse social classes, and they manifested a variety of spiritual gifts and powerful deeds that they could perform because they had had this experience of the Holy Spirit. They could do healings, speak in tongues, and practice prophecy. They shared certain common rituals, such as baptism and the Lord's Supper. We'll talk about both of those in a subsequent lecture.

However, his letters also show that from the beginning, Christians experienced severe disagreements about how this powerful experience of the Resurrection should have been translated into consistent patterns of behavior. Luke's idyllic portrayal in the chapters 2 and 4 of the Acts of the Apostles claims that all believers shared everything in common in Jerusalem's early church. Despite this, Paul's letters show us more of a historical reality. There was no golden moment of perfect unity in early Christianity. There was conflict from the beginning.

The New Testament, the Christian writings, is comprised of 27 compositions in Greek. They were written before the end of the first century, in response to the needs of these early communities. Because they were written in response to the needs and circumstances of these communities, the compositions of the New Testament are as diverse as the experiences and situations of the early Christians.

For the first Christians, *Scripture* obviously did not mean the New Testament. It wasn't written yet. *Scripture* meant the writings that they shared with their fellow Jews. The Jewish Scripture which they now read in the light of a crucified and raised messiah. They referred to it as *graffe*, or "writing." It was read out loud in the Christian assembly as it was in Jewish gatherings.

The distinctive Christian writings consist of letters. Thirteen are attributed to the Apostle Paul. Two are attributed to Peter, another Apostle; and three to John, another Apostle. One each is attributed to James and Jude, who may have been Apostles. There is also an anonymous treatise called "to the Hebrews," and an historical narrative concerning the first generation called the Acts of the Apostles. Finally, there is a visionary composition called The Book of Revelation.

These writings concentrate on the life and practices of the church. Acts gives an account of the earliest expansion of the church, and reveals the complexity and the energy of this early Christian movement. In them, Jesus appears mainly as a present and powerful Lord, although allusions are made to his human example as an important norm for Christians. For example, Paul tells the Corinthians to live by the mind of the Messiah. He tells the Galatians that they should live by the law of Christ. Clearly, the human Jesus is important even for those who celebrate him now as the powerful Lord.

Most people are impressed by the other four writings in the New Testament. These are the four narratives called Gospels. They are attributed in probable chronological sequence to Mark, Matthew, Luke, and John. They provide a rich collection of Jesus's sayings and deeds, as remembered by these communities over decades of oral transmission. These communities now believed in him as the "Lord of Creation;" that is, they remembered him in light of the Resurrection experience.

The evangelists—Matthew, Mark, Luke, and John—gathered these community traditions and put them together in the form of narratives. These narratives tell and retell the story of Jesus in a manner that instructs their readers in the life of discipleship. This is the distinctive Christian term for an adherent, or a follower. It means, interestingly enough, a learner; a *mathetes*, a "disciple," is somebody who learns. Thus, these gospel narratives invite readers to picture themselves as Jesus's human followers during his ministry, and as those who are learning from Jesus's words from his example, as he moves toward his death. Although Matthew, Luke, and Mark were using shared traditions, and although the writings are literarily interdependent, they are called the synoptic Gospels because they are so similar that they can be put in three parallel columns. Mark was probably the first Gospel, and was written around the year 70. Then Matthew and Luke each used Mark in composing their versions, and employed other traditions as well. They were probably written around the year 85.

Despite the shared traditions, and despite their literary interdependence, what is remarkable about these accounts is that they give really quite diverse portrayals of Jesus. He is not a cardboard figure, but is a complex and compelling personality in these four Gospels. In Mark, he appears as an attractive and yet repelling powerful wonder-worker who dies tragically, and his followers don't understand him at all. In Matthew, he is the pedagogue, the teacher of the church. In Luke, he is the prophetic person who calls the outcasts to share in his life. In John's Gospel, the strangest of them all, he is a revealer from the God who brings light into the world; he reveals that the world that resists God is full of darkness.

Therefore, although they have much in common, each of these Gospels also contains distinctive portrayals of Jesus. It is equally remarkable that even though these Gospels are written from the perspective of faith and perceive Jesus as the "Resurrected One," they render Jesus as a first-century Palestinian Jew with remarkable accuracy. Our shared last century is one of astounding archaeological discoveries. We have learned more about the world of antiquity than any other humans have ever known. We know more about first century Palestine than anybody has ever known before us. What is most remarkable is that the more we learn about first century Palestine, the more Jesus's words and deeds make sense within that context. He is unmistakably a Palestinian Jew of the first century.

We have learned in this lecture that Jesus is not the founder of Christianity in an obvious way. He did not create the church. The church was born out of the experiences and convictions of followers after his death; these experiences and convictions convinced those followers that he was not simply a dead guy of the past, but a powerful presence of their present, and they continue to succeed in convincing others in the present day as well.

Second Century and Self-Definition
Lecture 3

Jesus of Nazareth both is, and is not, the founder of Christianity.

In the beginning of the 2nd century of the common era, Christianity was an identifiable presence across the Roman Empire whose development was natural and organic but also bore the marks of its first creative expansion. The most obvious feature was the dominance of Gentile Christianity and of Greco-Roman culture. Christianity was more successful in attracting Gentiles than Jews, and after the Jewish War of 67–70, Jewish Christians were less visible. Sociologically and symbolically, Christian churches resembled Greco-Roman schools more than Jewish synagogues. As communities began to exchange and collect their writings, the question of how Christianity did or did not connect to Judaism was inevitable. The Christian martyr Justin's dialogue with the Jew Trypho, written around 135 A.D., marks the last face-to-face encounter of Christianity and Judaism for a long time.

The sparse literature of the early 2nd century reveals a movement that was diverse and sometimes divided, concerned for moral teaching and practice, and eager to offer a defense against attackers. Bishops (such as Ignatius and Polycarp) emerge as intellectual and moral leaders of communities, but the voice of prophecy was still alive (Hermas). Letters written between communities show less concern for doctrine or theology than for moral behavior and unity (see 1 Clement). The danger of being Christian is revealed by martyrdom (see Ignatius and Polycarp) and apologetic literature (Diognetus, Justin).

The second half of the 2nd century generated forms of diversity that challenged the Christian movement in fundamental ways and demanded a more explicit form of self-definition. A strong tendency toward cosmic dualism and religious asceticism appeared in the 2nd century in a variety of forms. It is not entirely an internal Christian phenomenon, although its effects on Christianity are impressive. It is not entirely "heterodox" in character, being found as well in popular Christian writings that do not challenge common convictions (see Infancy Gospel of James, Acts of Paul). The blanket term *Gnosticism* covers a wide range of Christian ascetical and dualistic tendencies that powerfully challenge the nature of the religious movement.

One form of the challenge moved in the direction of contracting traditional texts and tenets. The Assyrian apologist Tatian advocated a complete rejection of the world through an ascetic lifestyle. He proposed the *Diatesseron* as a single witness, instead of the four Gospels. Marcion of Sinope proposed a radical dualism that identified the God of the Old Testament with evil and, in his *Antitheses*, called for the rejection of the Old Testament and all of the New Testament except 10 letters of Paul and a shortened version of Luke's Gospel.

Another strongly ascetical tendency moved in the direction of expanding the courses of authority. Our knowledge of this tendency derives both from the descriptions of ancient opponents and from the Nag-Hammadi library, discovered in 1947. Both Sethian and Valentinian forms of Gnostic teaching challenged traditional teaching in favor of continuing revelation

Constantine was the first Christian emperor. His conversion and edict of toleration (the Edict of Milan in 313) reversed the political and cultural fortunes of Christianity.

and produced a plethora of "inspired" literature that contained an ascetic ideology. The challenge of new teachers, new teaching, and new scripture was both frontal and massive. It proposed a version of Christianity that was individualistic and opposed to the order of creation.

The orthodox party took its stand on a *canon of scripture* that consisted of the Old Testament and 27 writings of the New Testament.

The response of orthodox teachers to this complex challenge had profound consequences for the shape of Christianity through the centuries. The production of "anti-heretical" literature by such leaders as Irenaeus of Lyons, Tertullian, and Clement of Alexandria emphasized the importance of "right thinking" (orthodoxy) within this religious tradition. Irenaeus, in particular, developed (in his *Against Heresies*) a well-balanced response to the Gnostic challenge. Rather than a truncated or expanded collection of writings, the orthodox party took its stand on a *canon of scripture* that consisted of the Old Testament and 27 writings of the New Testament. Rather than a widely diverse set of myths, the orthodox party insisted on a *rule of faith* that defined traditional beliefs. Rather than many inspired teachers, the orthodox party claimed an *apostolic succession* of public leaders, called the bishops, who maintained tradition. The strategy of self-definition used in the battle with Gnosticism became standard for later internal conflicts: Bishops gathered in council to study Scripture and elaborate the creed.

At the beginning of the 3rd century, Christianity was internally prepared for its long period of political and cultural influence that began with Constantine in 313 C.E. The process of self-definition was not only conceptual: The church that emerged was embodied, public, institutional, and ritual, in character. The communion among the orthodox bishops made them visible leaders in the empire, while protest forms of Christianity sought refuge outside the empire. ■

Essential Reading

"The Letters of Ignatius of Antioch," in *The Apostolic Fathers*, translated by Kirsopp Lake (Loeb Classical Library; Cambridge: Harvard University Press, 1915).

"The Gospel of Truth," in *The Gnostic Scriptures*, translated by Bentley Layton (Garden City: Doubleday, 1987).

Irenaeus of Lyons, *Against Heresies*, in *The Ante-Nicene Fathers: The Writings of the Fathers Down to A.D. 325*, edited by A. Roberts and J. Donaldson, revised by A. C. Coxe (Peabody, MA: Hendrickson Publishers, 1994).

Supplemental Reading

P. Carrington, *The Early Christian Church*, vol. 2: *The Second Christian Century* (Cambridge: Cambridge University Press, 1957).

W. H. Wagner, *After the Apostles: Christianity in the Second Century* (Minneapolis: Fortress Press, 1994).

Questions to Consider

1. What would Christianity have become had the movements led by Marcion and Valentinus been victorious?

2. Comment on this proposition: "Second-century conflicts were battles over ideas with nothing important at stake."

Second Century and Self-Definition
Lecture 3—Transcript

We have seen that Christianity was not born out of a carefully developed program by Jesus of Nazareth, but by the conviction that this executed criminal was the resurrected Lord, and the "Life-Giving Spirit" among his followers.

In our last lecture, we caught a glimpse of earliest Christianity in its first years. We saw how it moved across the Roman Empire from Jerusalem to Rome—establishing dozens of small communities, managing five major transitions as it did from the beginning, writing letters, engaging in certain shared practices, and experiencing persecution from without and divisions already from within.

In this lecture, I want to look at our next identifiable historical moment, namely the second century. I want to show you that it is in the second century that Christianity really defined itself as a new and distinct religion, rather than as a sect of Judaism.

In the beginning of the second century of the C.E., Christianity had become an identifiable presence in the Roman Empire. Its development was natural and organic, but also bore the marks of its first creative expansion.

The most obvious thing that strikes us when we look at Christianity in the early years of the second century is the dominance of Gentile Christianity over Jewish Christianity, and of Greco-Roman culture on Christianity.

From the beginning, Christianity had been much more successful at drawing Gentiles into its ranks than it had Jews, and there was an increased difficulty in appealing to fellow Jews. For example, in his letter to the Romans around the year 57, Paul engages in a long argument in which he hopes for—and expects—the conversion of his fellow Jews even during his lifetime. This is in Romans, chapters 9 to 11. However, Luke looks back on the Jewish mission as pretty much over 30 years later. The final words of his hero, Paul, in the Acts of the Apostles are, "This word of salvation has been sent to the Gentiles. They will believe."

There was a combination of rejection by Christians' fellow Jews, and acceptance by Gentiles. Indeed, it can be argued that one of the reasons for Christianity's rapid expansion and success is that it rode on the back of Judaism. It offered to Gentiles a more accessible and less arduous form of Judaism, because it didn't require circumcision and the observance of the law. It was popular among Gentiles but not among Jews. For Jews, Jesus was a failed and possibly false messiah, cursed by God because of the means of his death.

Furthermore, Christians were not loyal to Judaism. In the Jewish War against Rome during the years 67 to 70, the small Christian community in Jerusalem departed. It left the city before the final and climactic battle that led to the burning of the city and the destruction of the Temple.

There was also rejection from the Jewish side. Sometime around the year 85, Jewish synagogues developed what is called the "Nineteenth Benediction," or the *Bikat Ha-Minim,* the "Benediction against Heretics." It forbade those who proclaimed two powers in heaven to be part of their worship, so in effect Christians were excluded from the synagogue as well.

So sociologically and symbolically, in the early second century, Christian churches resembled Greco-Roman philosophical schools, which were well organized and followed a common way of life and teachings, more than they did the Jewish synagogue. The major impact from the synagogue was in the forms of worship in early Christianity: the reading of *Corda*, the reading of Scripture, the prayers, and the use of psalms and hymns. These all came not from the side of Greco-Roman culture, but from the side of Jewish culture. These were philosophical schools, which as you remember were well organized and followed a common way of life and teachings, and so forth.

As Christian communities began to exchange and collect their writings, this was an important step toward Christianity becoming a common thing. That is, churches that received letters from Paul exchanged them with other communities and got their letters, sort of the way we traded comic books when we were kids. In this way, a collection of texts was formed that gave early Christians a kind of common library; this began really right after the death of Paul. As they began to collect and exchange their writings, the question of how they should relate themselves to Judaism was both pressing and pretty much predetermined.

Christianity was going away from Judaism. Indeed, it is in *Justin's* dialogue with Trypho, written around the year 135 that we find our last serious face-to-face exchange between a Christian and a Jew on a fairly equal basis. The year 135 is significant because this was when Jerusalem was finally destroyed by the Romans, following the Bar-Kokhba revolt. Trypho, the Jewish leader, encountered Justin, and they had a several-day conversation in which, revealingly, the topics revolved mainly around which version of Scripture is better, the Hebrew Bible or the Greek translation. Trypho said the Hebrew version was, and Justin said the Greek translation was.

In relation to that, how do the prophecies of the prophets unfold? Are they fulfilled in Jesus or not? Obviously, Trypho and Justin disagree about that as well. That is really the last gasp of a face-to-face encounter between Christianity and Judaism for a long time, and Christianity becomes more and more Gentile.

The sparse literature of the early second century reveals a movement that was diverse and sometimes divided. It was concerned with moral teaching and practice rather than theological speculation, and was eager to offer a defense against attackers. We see the emergence of bishops. The term "bishop," *episcopos,* means a "superintendent," and we see strong leaders like Ignatius of Antioch and Polycarp of Smyrna, who emerge as intellectual and moral leaders of communities. Ignatius of Antioch wrote letters to seven churches across Asia Minor as he was being transported on his way to Rome to be executed, instructing them on how they should live.

Polycarp also collected the letters of Ignatius and then added a further letter of his own, in which basically he pulled together the teachings of Ignatius and Paul and communicated them to the church in Philippa.

These intellectual and moral leaders, these bishops, represented a kind of an institutional Christianity, but the voice of prophecy was not yet entirely dead. *The Shepherd of Hermas* was written in the city of Rome, in which a simple layperson received visions from God and challenged the wealthy, calling them to a life of poverty. The early writing, *The Teaching of the Twelve Apostles*, the *Didache*, gives instructions on how visiting prophets are to be received by communities. There still was some sense of itinerant prophetic activity in the church in the early second century, but more and more Christianity appeared as an organization that was given to a kind of a domestication, moral teaching, and so forth. It didn't have a concern for doctrine or theology so much as it did good behavior.

Polycarp's letter to the Philippians weaves together those passages from the Apostle Paul that deal not with theology, but with how people are to live in the household and the assembly—how they are to take care of widows and so forth.

Clement of Rome writing around the year 95 to the church in Corinth—a church to which Paul himself had written—takes up the theme of harmony, unity, and good behavior in the assembly, in opposition to movements of rivalry and envy, which were causing dissension in that community.

Christianity, if you will, was very moralistic in the beginning of this second century. It was also a dangerous profession. There were sporadic and increasing persecutions of the Christian movement as it became more popular and gained more adherents, beginning with a very small touch with Nero in the year 64. There were subsequent persecutions under the Emperors Domitian, Trajan, and Marcus Aurelius in the second century. This meant that martyrdom, bearing witness even to death, being executed by the Roman authorities, was not infrequent among these early Christians. Both Ignatius and Polycarp were martyrs.

Persecution also stimulated the development of apologetic literature written by Christians in the early second century. The word "apologetic" comes from the Greek word *apologia* which means "a defense." Apologetic literature is fascinating because it is the effort by a group that is counter-cultural to explain itself to the larger culture. In order to do that, however, it must use the terms of the larger culture. This means that even as it's showing how "we're just like you," it also functions as a means of self-definition. By portraying ourselves in the language of others, we also become assimilated to the language of others.

We have a lovely composition called the *Letter of Diognetus*. We don't even know who Diognetus was, but it was written around the middle of the century to the Emperor Antoninus Pius; he probably never read it, but it portrays Christians in remarkable fashion as being just like everybody else in the world. Diognetus says that we don't dress differently, we don't act differently, and we don't eat strange foods, but that we are the soul of the world—an image that says that Christians are in some sense the life-giving ferment of society.

We have the apology written by Justin, the same person who entered into disputation with Trypho the Jew. In the apology, Justin portrays Christianity as a philosophical school, in terms that would be intelligible to the wider Greco-Roman culture.

All of this was happening in the first half of the second century. It is the second half of the second century that generated forms of diversity within the Christian movement. It challenged Christianity in fundamental ways and demanded a more explicit form of self-definition. In the second century, there was a strong tendency toward cosmic dualism and religious asceticism in a variety of forms.

Cosmic dualism is a view of reality in which two powers are pretty much on an equal plane and competing with each other. For example, there was "good" and there was "evil." In the second century, good was pretty much lined up with spirit, and evil was pretty much lined up with physical reality or materiality.

"Asceticism" means "discipline," and comes from the Greek word *ascesis*, which simply means "discipline." "Asceticism," then, means "self-control," especially in sexual matters and in dietary matters.

When asceticism is connected to cosmic dualism, it obviously implies that by controlling physical reality, one cultivates the spirit and diminishes the impact of the physical.

This broad movement of asceticism and cosmic dualism was not unique to Christianity in the second century. It appears in Greco-Roman literature, in the Hermetic literature, in Jewish literature, and in early mystical texts such as the Hekhalot literature, but it is in Christianity that its influence is most impressive, and almost redefines this movement.

It is not entirely heterodox or heretical in character. We find traces of this cosmic dualism and this asceticism in popular Christian writings, which otherwise do not challenge the common convictions in any fundamental way. These were eagerly read by Christians as part of their recreational literature, if you will.

Let me give you two examples. One is the Infancy Gospel of James, which was written around the year 150, and is remarkable for its attention to the mother of Jesus, Mary. It is this gospel that places a particular importance upon Mary's biological virginity, even after the birth of Jesus. Clearly, there was a kind of an obsession with virginity, as opposed to active sexuality. The Infancy Gospel of James, by the way, is where we get the tradition that Joseph was an old man. That's how Joseph was portrayed, that Mary was a young girl who was Joseph's ward, and that they weren't really married in any real sense of the term. It was this apocryphal writing which really became the source for much of Christian iconography through the ages. It doesn't come from the canonical gospels, but from the Infancy Gospel of James.

Another writing is the Acts of Paul and Thecla. This writing is dated around the year 180. Paul is portrayed as identifying the Resurrection with a life of virginity, and Thecla, the heroine, abandons her fiancé to join Paul in a virginal way of life. They practice severe physical asceticism together with a life of virginity.

All of these writings were part of the Christian collection. It is when we turn to the blanket term *Gnosticism* that we find the powerful challenge to Christianity as a religious movement. *Gnosticism* covers a wide range of Christian ascetical and dualistic tendencies. These tendencies are connected to peculiar convictions concerning a revealed esoteric, secret, saving knowledge that applies only to some people and not others.

One form of this dualism moved in the direction of contracting traditional texts and tenets. The Assyrian teacher Tatian, for example, wrote a powerful apology called *Against the Greeks*, in which he chastised the Greeks for their polytheism and their immoral way of life. However, he was equally scandalized by the fact that there were four Christian gospels. He thought that that plurality didn't make sense, and so he wanted to create a single gospel harmony. He wrote a book called the *Diatesseron*, which in Greek means "through the four," and he wove together the four gospels into a single life of Jesus. He also advocated a form of Christianity in which everybody had to be a virgin in order to be a Christian.

Even more influential was a teacher called Marcion. Around the year 150, he was a failed candidate for the bishopric of Rome. In a high dudgeon, he went off and formed his own form of Christianity, which was profoundly dualistic. For Marcion, the world is equally divided between good and evil. Evil is all lined up on the side of physical reality, and good is all lined up on the side of spirit.

The implication of this is that the creator God of the Old Testament, the God of the Jews, is an evil God, because he created materiality. Jesus, for Marcion, was a liberator from the body. Therefore, there has to be an absolute division between Jesus and his followers, and Judaism. It is Marcion, and his book *Antitheses*, who develops a stereotype which many Christians have never lost: The evil God of justice, the angry God of the Old Testament, over against the loving God represented by Jesus, and has nothing to do with Judaism.

Logically, then, Marcion advocated a reduction of the Christian canon. It would consist only of the 10 letters of Paul. Paul was the only one who got

Jesus right for Marcion. In addition, there was an expurgated version of the Gospel of Luke. Marcion thought Paul meant the Gospel of Luke when Paul said "My Gospel." Therefore, we have only 10 of Paul's letters, and only one Gospel. Marcion therefore thought that Christianity could have only one theological position. That one position was that to be a Christian you needed to be a virgin, you needed to be ascetical, and you needed to flee the world of materiality; to be a Christian meant that you had to be a person of the spirit and not of the body. Tatian and Marcion moved in the direction of reduction simultaneously, and this is why the crisis was so complex.

Simultaneously, the movement of Gnosticism expanded the sources of authority within Christianity. Our knowledge of Gnosticism derives mainly from the writings of Christians against the Gnostic teachers. These include writers such as Irenaeus and Tertullian; they give us long citations and descriptions of their teachings.

For a long time, that's all we had, but then in 1947 at Nag Hammadi in Egypt, we discovered an entire library of Gnostic writings. They included a bizarre collection of gospels, revelatory texts, and tractates. Some of them clearly have no connection with Christianity. Some of them are deeply hostile to Judaism, and some are not so hostile to Judaism.

From both these outsider sources and insider sources, we have a better view now of how powerful this movement really was. Sethian Gnosticism is explicitly hostile to Judaism, explicitly hostile to the creator God. Valentinian Gnosticism is slightly less hostile toward Judaism. Both of them challenged traditional Christian teaching in favor of a continuing revelation that is contained in "inspired" writings, and contained an ascetic ideology.

Gnostics divided humanity into three categories: the Gnostics, "pneumatic," who were the elite and who alone would be saved, the psychic, who had possibilities if they could be converted to Gnosticism, and the "hylic," the mud people who had no future at all. In the Gnostics' view, the people who went to the ordinary Christian churches were largely the hylic; they had a few psychic among them from whom they could get to their followers.

Gnosticism fundamentally is a highly individualistic, highly mystical, highly elitist form of Christianity. It proposes new teachings, new teachers, and new scriptures that encompass the traditional teachings but reinterpret them in a fundamental way. Christianity becomes a matter of "only the smart get saved," to put it in really simple terms. In order to be a true believer, the practices of Christianity were not those of the body, but rather of those that fled the body so that severe asceticism was required both sexually and in diet. Indeed, "anorexia" is sort of the body language of Gnosticism. The less you have of the body the more you have of the spirit.

This was a powerful challenge. There were times in the second century when the followers of Tatian, of Marcion, and of Valentines probably numerically outnumbered those of the party we now call the Orthodox, those who were the "mud people," if you will. It was such a challenge because it was not simply a matter of new teachers and new texts, but rather a fundamental ideological challenge, which moved Christianity from being a public and embodied tradition to one that was esoteric, mystical, and individualistic.

The response of teachers like Tertullian, Irenaeus and Clement of Alexandria, whom we now call Orthodox in the obviously biased description of "right-thinking" or "right-teaching," had profound consequences for the shape of Christianity through the centuries. Tertullian was in North Africa, Clement of Alexandria was in the city of Alexandria in Egypt, and Irenaeus was a bishop of Lyon in France.

They wrote massive works in rebuttal of this Gnostic tendency, and the volume of their writings indicates to us how important literacy was among these Christians and how much intellectual labor was going into all of these things, despite the fact that there was still martyrdom and persecution going on. There was lively intellectual debate. Irenaeus in particular developed a well-balanced response to the mass Gnostic challenge, in his book *Against Heresies*, Book III.

Rather than on a truncated or expanded collection of writings, Irenaeus took his stand on a *canon of Scripture* that included all of the Old Testament, and the 27 writings of the New Testament. He did this not because these writings were inspired, but because they represented the sense of what the church really was.

Notice that Christianity, therefore, set itself in a position of a continuing dialogue with Judaism. Christians did not rewrite the Old Testament in the way that the Qur'an does; it did not retell that story. Rather, the Christian writings form an appendix to the Old Testament.

The second element of Irenaeus' strategy was to oppose this wide variety of myths that were developed by the Gnostics with what was called a *rule of faith*, a set of propositions, which functioned to guide the reading of Scripture. This is what later became the *Creed*. This is the *Profession of Faith,* which states how Christians see reality; even the most adventuresome theologian in the Orthodox party or Origen of Alexandria in the late second and early third century began his adventure in speculative theology by recounting those teachings that he shared in common with all other Christians, before entering into his systematic theology.

Thirdly, and very significantly, Irenaeus proposed the *apostolic succession*, as opposed to the secret teachers. We have now a canon, rather than expanded writings. We have a *rule of faith*, rather than myths, and we have a tradition of teachers. Irenaeus demonstrated this *apostolic succession* by tracing the bishops of Rome back from his own time to Saint Peter. In so doing, he shows us the importance of the Roman church already in the late second century. It was regarded by Irenaeus and others as the most important of the churches.

Irenaeus' strategy of self-definition that he used in the battle with Gnosticism became standard for later internal conflicts within Christianity. Whenever there would be a crisis within Christianity, public institutional figures—such as the bishops and the *apostolic succession*—would gather in council, read the canon of Scriptures, and on that basis elaborate the Creed, *rule of faith*. This is the way that Christians responded to subsequent crises.

At the beginning of the third century, Christianity was internally prepared for its long period of political and cultural influence that began with Constantine in 313 C.E. This is the year when Constantine issued the Edict of Milan; this changed Christianity from being a persecuted minority to being the official religion of the Roman Empire.

This process of self-definition was not simply conceptual. The church that emerged out of the debate with Gnosticism was embodied. Christianity really values the body. Christianity notoriously has had problems with sex, and what to do with sexuality, but it has always affirmed the importance of marriage and the importance of having children. At that level, at least, it countered the view of Gnosticism, which thought of sexuality as collaboration and evil and having children as the perpetuation of evil materiality.

Christianity has remained embodied and public. It includes potentially all people—not just the smart, not just the elite; hoy-poloy belong to the Christian movement.

It is institutional in character, in that it has visible leaders, rather than secret and charismatic rulers. These official leaders may not be terribly bright themselves, but nevertheless they are networked with each other in a form of organization.

Finally, Christianity is ritual in character, because bodies matter. The way bodies perform certain kinds of actions together is important. Space and time matter because bodies matter.

This communion among Orthodox bishops, finally, made them the visible leaders within the Empire in this community, so that when Constantine made Christianity the official religion of the Empire, it was these Orthodox leaders, not the secret teachers, who were going to be an important body of people to interact with.

We find, then, in subsequent centuries, the fact that Orthodox Christianity tended to be the imperial Christianity. Heterodox forms of Christianity tended to flourish outside the boundaries of the Roman Empire—in East Syria, in Egypt, and in North Africa. At the end of the second century, Christianity was internally prepared to take on the burden of being the imperial religion.

The Christian Story
Lecture 4

Christianity is both deeply historical and mythical in its way of seeing the world. History and myth come together in the Christian story, which provides a comprehensive narrative that extends from the creation of the world to the end of time.

To be Christian means to share a story about the world from beginning to end. The "story character" of Christianity is one of the consequences of the conflict with Gnosticism, because story bears implications concerning the significance of physical bodies and time. Part of that story is found in texts shared with Judaism (the Old Testament); part is found in the distinctive Christian scriptures (the New Testament); and part, in the developments of the religion over a 2,000-year existence.

The Christian story combines three distinct aspects of temporality: the historical, the mythical, and the eschatological. Christians claim the historical character of much of the story told in the Bible, especially the part concerning Jesus. Yet the designation of *myth* is appropriate for other parts of the story (see the primordial origins) and for all of the story in part (see the transcendental claim made for empirical events). Christians also struggle with the notion of *eschatology* (literally, "last things"), both with respect to the future and the present.

The Christian story before Jesus is understood as a time of anticipation and promise. Christians share with Jews the accounts of creation, the tales of the Patriarchs, the saga of the Exodus and Conquest, the recital of kings, of exiles, and of restorations, but read them from a different perspective. For Jews, the center of Scripture is the revelation of God's Law at Sinai, while for Christians, it is the revelation of God through human and social events. Christians see the ancient story as providing the basic framework for a relationship between God and humans (the covenant) and as a promise that leads to a historical climax in the coming of the Messiah. In particular,

Christians read the prophetic literature, not only in terms of the ancient social and religious criticism leveled by the Jewish prophets, but also in terms of the prediction of Jesus as Messiah. Christians, like Jews, read Amos and Jeremiah and Isaiah as powerful voices of reform, calling Israel to faithfulness to the covenant. Unlike Jews, they see many passages in Jeremiah, Isaiah, Ezekiel, and Daniel as having their fuller meaning in the future.

> **The Christian story combines three distinct aspects of temporality: the historical, the mythical, and the eschatological.**

Christians see Jesus both as the fulfillment of prophecy and as the inauguration of God's rule. In his human ministry, Jesus announces the "rule of God" and symbolizes its power through his works of healing and exorcism. By his Resurrection, Jesus shares God's rule as "Lord" over the church and even the cosmos. The earliest Christian writings conceive of the story in terms of an "already and not yet." The Resurrection of Jesus is the "first fruits" of a cosmic victory that has still not been fully realized. The *parousia* (Second Coming) of Jesus will represent God's final triumph over sin and death.

Christians approach the 2,000-year-long story of the church from multiple perspectives. Christians agree on dividing Christian history into discrete stages that combine religious and secular dimensions: apostolic, patristic, medieval, Renaissance, Reformation, Enlightenment, modern, contemporary. The religious or theological assessment of the discrete periods is, however, controverted among Christians.

Christians share the conviction that their story has a goal, but they have less agreement concerning what that goal is. The notion of the "age to come" or the "world to come" has fluctuated in its importance at different periods of Christianity's history. Even Christians with a strong sense of eschatology have a variety of versions of what the future holds. ■

Essential Reading

Book of Revelation.

Gospel of Matthew.

Paul's First Letter to the Thessalonians.

Supplemental Reading

R. M. Grant, with David Tracy, *A Short History of the Interpretation of the Bible*, 2nd revised and enlarged edition (Philadelphia: Fortress Press, 1984).

J. L. Kugel and R.A. Greer, *Early Biblical Interpretation* (Library of Early Christianity; Philadelphia: Westminster Press, 1986).

Questions to Consider

1. In light of this presentation, consider what elements of the "Christian story" are best designated as *myth*, *history*, or *eschatology*.

2. Compare and contrast the understanding of *Scripture* held respectively by Jews, Christians, and Muslims.

The Christian Story
Lecture 4—Transcript

Now, we have gained some sense of how Christianity began—not with what Jesus did during his lifetime, but with experiences and convictions concerning him by his followers after his death, called his Resurrection.

We've learned how Christianity gained a foothold in the Roman Empire in the first 70 years of its existence, how it survived persecution from without and dissention from within from the beginning, and above all how it defined itself as a new and distinctive religion. It was communal and public in character, against the individualizing and dualistic tendencies of Gnosticism in the middle of the second century.

We can leave diachronic developments alone for a moment. The next significant event is going to be the Edict of Milan in 313, which transformed Christianity from a persecuted minority to the established religion of the Roman Empire.

Let's leave that development for a moment and move to some synchronic or synthetic lectures that introduce us to the basic elements of Christianity as a religion. These are the elements that all of its manifestations share to one degree or another. These are the things that Christians hold in common.

We begin with the Christian story from creation to "the world to come." At the very least, to be Christian means to share a certain story about the world—from the world's beginning to the world's end. The "story character" of Christianity, if you will, is actually one of the consequences of the conflict with Gnosticism. A story bears implications concerning the significance of physical bodies in time. Time, after all, is simply the movement of physical bodies in space, or the measurement of physical bodies in space.

The Gnostic myths of the middle of the second century were not properly stories at all. Rather, they were descriptions of the divine elements. They were a sort of heavenly or divine furniture or architecture in which nothing fundamentally changed, because they were removed from bodies.

Christianity's affirmation of the body is also an affirmation of time; it is also therefore an affirmation of narrator and human narrator as meaningful. It's one of the distinguishing characteristics of Christianity among the world's religions, and it also means, of course, that it establishes continuity with creation and with the God of creation, which is the God of the Jews.

For Christians to share a story means that they see themselves as creatures of the earth, and of having a destiny somehow together with the earth. Part of the Christian story is found in the texts that they share with Jews. These texts are called by Jews the Tanakh (TaNaK.) They are made up of Torah, the five books of Moses; Nevi'im and the Prophets, which include both historical books and the classical prophets; and the Ketuvim, the Writings or Wisdom traditions.

The Tanakh are the same compositions that Christians call the Old Testament. Part of the Christian story is found in those texts. Part of the Christian story is found in the distinctive Christian writings of the New Testament, the 27 compositions in Greek that I described in an earlier lecture. Part of the story is found in the developments of Christianity over its 2,000-year existence. Finally, part of the story still has to be told. Part of the story of Christianity is its vision of the future.

Christianity's story combines—in complex ways—three different aspects of temporality, or perhaps better, narratives: the historical, the mythic, and the eschatological.

Let me take them in turn. Historical has to do with events that take place in the empirical realm, human events in time and space, which are at least potentially verifiable by empirical means of measurement and description. World War II is an obvious historical event by that kind of designation.

Mythic narrative does not mean fictional or untrue, but more properly, it means events that happen in the empirical realm and that go beyond the empirical realm. That is to say that they somehow involve supernatural or divine agency. Any story that involves God is going to be mythic in that sense, because God is obviously not an object that is empirically verifiable.

Take, as an example, a healing. That somebody is healed from an illness is, or can be, an historical event. It can be empirically described. You're sick one moment; you're not the next. But to call that healing a miracle is to speak mythically.

The final category is eschatological. The word "eschatological" comes from the Greek word *eschaton*, which means "last things." But in Christianity, this is a very complex category, because it means the end of the story sometimes, but it also has implications about the goal of the story, and even the quality of the entire story. I'll try to unpack this a little bit as I go along.

Let's look at the various parts of the Christian story under these three kinds of notions: the historical, the mythical, and the eschatological.

Christians claim that much of their story is historical. This includes the story that is told in the Bible, including the Old Testament. Christians consider Abraham, Moses, and David to be real figures in ancient Israel, and not simply fictional creatures. Even though it is difficult to determine exactly what they did historically, they are nevertheless available for historical analysis. Likewise, they consider prophets like Amos and Isaiah to be real characters who interacted with the Israelite kings, and not simply literary devices for the delivery of poetry.

Christians especially consider the part of the biblical story having to do with Jesus as historical. I mentioned in an earlier lecture how difficult it is to get at the historical Jesus in any full sense of the term; this is because of the character of the narratives that talk about Jesus. Their perspective comes from the point of view of the Resurrection. Nonetheless, all Christians consider that Jesus is a real historical figure. Christianity for them is not born out of a mushroom cult, or some other hallucinogen, or a mass hysteria. Jesus is a real figure in first-century Palestine. His death is real. This is important. It is a real historical event, the death of Jesus. Indeed, the death of Jesus under Pontius Pilate is perhaps the single most historically verifiable thing about the figure of Jesus.

By and large, Christians think that what the Gospels report about Jesus is also historical. That is, he really did work wonders. He really did preach. He really did speak in parables. Although most critical Christians will recognize that it's difficult to reconstruct his teachings and his actions, nevertheless they do not think of them as events that were simply fabricated by the evangelists.

So much of the Christian story in the Bible itself is regarded by Christians as historical, yet the language of myth is also obviously pertinent, for parts of the story. Clearly, the story of the creation of the world in Genesis must be called mythic. It is not natural science. It is not empirical research, but rather the story of God creating all things visible and invisible by his word alone. This has this mythic character to it.

The term *myth* also applies to dimensions of the story as a whole. To say that Jesus of Nazareth is a real Jewish figure of the first century is a perfectly good historical claim. But to state, as Paul does, that God was in Christ reconciling the world to God's self is mythic language. There is nothing empirically verifiable in that statement. When the Gospel of John says that "The word became flesh and dwelt among us," that clearly is mythic language, not historical language. Thus, the Christian story involved dimensions both of the historical and the mythic.

Christians also struggle with the notion of *eschatology*, "last things." Is it simply what is going to happen in the future, or is it also something that is happening in the present? In other words, as Christians themselves live out their lives today in the beginning of the 21st century, are they in the same realm of temporality as everybody else? Are they simply living within history, or are they also participating already in eternity? That is, are they also taking part in another realm simultaneously, which we might call eschatology? In other words, is eschatology simply a matter of the future, or is it also a quality of the present? Christianity is very complex in its story.

Let's begin to look, then, at the various moments in this story as Christians tell it. As I said, Christians share with Jews the five books of Moses; these have the account of the creation by God, by a word. Above all, they have (for Christians) humans' betrayal of God and disobedience of God through sin. This happens with the very first humans, Adam and Eve. Additionally, in the books of Moses, we find the stories of the patriarchs: Abraham, with whom God tried to restore relationship to humanity through the covenant of circumcision and by giving a promise of a blessing; and Abraham's children: Isaac, his child Jacob, and Joseph.

Then, there is the story of the great saga of the Exodus, of the liberation of the people of Israel from slavery under Moses, and the conquest of the land of Canaan for Israel's own. There are the narratives and the sagas of the kings of Israel and of Judah; these are recounted in the books of Samuel, Kings and Chronicles. There is the story of Israel's exile because of its idolatrous ways to Assyria, to Babylon, and to Egypt. There are the stories of the return from exile that are told in the books of Nehemiah and Ezra.

Christians read all of this as part of their story as well as the story of the Jews. Christians, in other words, insert themselves into the story of Judaism. When Paul is writing to Gentile converts in Corinth in the year 54, he says, "Our fathers who are in the desert." He simply makes the generation of the wilderness the immediate predecessors of the Christians.

Yet even though Christians share all of these accounts, they read them differently, from a different perspective. For Jews, these stories find their center in the revelation of God's Law on Mount Sinai through Moses. When a Jew reads the Book of Exodus, for example, yes, the liberation from Egypt is terribly exciting and important, but the climax of the story is found in the giving of the law, including the long description of the building of the temple and of the worship that is to be carried out in the temple. Judaism, from the first century until today, bases itself upon that part of the biblical account.

For Christians, the focus is much more on how God was active in the plot itself—in the story of liberation, in the story of the conquests, and so forth. Above all, Christians focus in a quite different place than Jews when they look at Genesis.

In Judaism, there is no such thing as original sin, which marks all of humanity. Christians are obsessed with the very beginning of the story in Genesis—how humans are created in the image of God, and how they failed that image by disobedience. The notion of an original fall from grace—fall from God's favors—is fundamental to Christianity because everything else in the story then is seen in light of that fall.

In Judaism, that's simply not a focus. That's simply not an important part of the story.

Christians furthermore, then, see this story as providing the fundamental framework for a relationship with God, which is established by the creation of humans in God's image, which is broken by sin, by this disobedience, and then which God seeks to restore with humans through covenant—through establishing a relationship—first, with Abraham, through circumcision; and then, through Moses, with the revelation of the law, which tells people how they are to live in accordance with God's will.

Christians see all of this as the fundamental framework, but what they single out more than Jews do is the promise made to Abraham.

When Jews look at the story of Abraham, the tendency is to focus on the circumcision as the premise of the Jewish way of life. When Christians look at the story of Abraham, they look at the promise of the blessing that is to come upon all nations, Gentiles, and they see that promise to Abraham as being fulfilled in the Messiah—Jesus—and in the gift of the Holy Spirit that has been poured out on people after the Resurrection of Jesus.

Thus, even though Christians share all of this narrative material, they look at different things, emphasize different things, and read it from a very different perspective. In particular, Christians read the prophetic literature of Israel very differently, especially Daniel, Isaiah, Jeremiah, and Ezekiel—the four major prophets. They read them not only in terms of ancient social and religious criticism leveled by the Jewish prophets against corruption and idolatry within ancient Israel, but also in terms of foreshadowing or predicting the future and what will happen in Jesus, the "Anointed One."

To be sure, Christians, like Jews, read the prophets Amos and Jeremiah and Isaiah as powerful voices of reform, as voices that criticize the worship of other gods in ancient Israel, and the manifestation of that worship in social oppression in which the rich triumph over the poor, and the prophets' call to return to covenant, to return to this relationship with God, which is expressed not in ritual worship, but in social justice. Christians share that reading of the prophets with Jews, and in contemporary Christianity that reading of the prophets has been very, very important. We'll talk more about that later when we talk about Christian morality.

From the beginning, however, unlike Jewish readers, they see in passages of Jeremiah, Isaiah, Ezekiel, and Daniel, deliverings and hints of their fuller meaning in the future. Christians think of the sayings of the prophets as being fulfilled in Jesus. In other words, these are open-ended texts, which point forward to a later historical realization.

Jeremiah 32, for example, has the prophet talking about a future, new covenant that God is going to create with humans—not a covenant of external observation, but a covenant written internally in part. This notion of a new covenant obviously runs all the way through the New Testament, which is another way of translating new covenant. There is this sense that what Jeremiah foretold is now happening. It is not a religion of external observance, but a religion of internal transformation. As Jeremiah said, "No man will have to say to his neighbor, seek the Lord, because everybody will seek the Lord internally." The prophet Isaiah, in chapters 52 and 53, speaks of a mysterious person, a servant, who suffers innocently on behalf of others. Because of that mysterious innocent suffering, other people are put in a right relationship with God.

There was no Jew of the first century who read that passage as being about a messiah, certainly not an individual messiah. They read it as being about Israel's triumph over other nations.

Christians, however, after the Resurrection and in light of the way that Jesus suffered and died, read Isaiah 52 and Isaiah 53 as virtually a script, which is enacted in the account of Jesus's suffering and death. Likewise, they saw in certain psalms, such as Psalm 22 and Psalm 69, indications of a person who is innocent, who is beset by enemies and oppressed and suffering, and even cries out, "My God, my God; why have you forsaken me?" Yet, he is approved by God and is vindicated by God.

These Psalms, 62 and 69, Isaiah 52 and 53, Jeremiah 32, and many other passages, were not read by Jews of the first century as foretelling a messiah, but were read by Christians in light of their experience of Jesus's death and Resurrection as pointing forward to their realization. The phrase "the fulfillment of prophecy" is a key phrase for Christians when they read what they now call the Old Testament, in light of their readings, which are a New Testament.

In this story, Christians see Jesus both as an end and a beginning. Jesus is the fulfillment of those prophecies, but is also the inauguration of God's rule. In his human ministry, Jesus announces the "rule of God," and symbolizes that power of God's rule through his works of healing and exorcism. Jesus is not seen by Christians as establishing a theocracy or sketching a system of social arrangements, but rather as calling for a reform of the heart, a reform of individual conscience, and of the formation of a community that lives in a certain way.

For Christians, the most important thing about the story of Jesus in his lifetime is not what he said and did. It is that in Jesus, God entered human existence. This is the doctrine called *Incarnation*, "becoming flesh." To use Hindu terms, Jesus is an *avatara* in that sense of the deities. He is an appearance, but not simply an appearance—a realization of God in human form. It is not what Jesus said and did, but who he was, that is so fundamental to Christians. In this sense, Christians resolve the mystery of suffering by having God participate in human suffering. Suffering is not alien to God's self.

By Jesus's Resurrection, furthermore, Jesus has entered into God's rule and God's triumph as a human person. He is Lord over the church and even over the cosmos, so that God's fundamental victory has already been won within history. The Resurrection in this sense for Christians, as I mentioned earlier, is analogous to creation itself. That's one of the reasons why Genesis is so important for Christians, because if Jesus is the beginning of a new creation, if he is a new Adam, obviously he is responding to the first creation, the first Adam. That's the way in which Christian theology has tended to play out the story in terms of that first human person, with Jesus as the new human person, the new human possibility.

It is obvious that God's triumph in history is not empirically visible. The earliest Christians thought in terms of an "already" and a "not yet," that there was a sense in which God's triumph in creation had been realized through the Resurrection of Jesus. Not only has God entered fully into humanity in the Incarnation; but, in the Resurrection, humanity now partakes fully in the divine. Yet, people still get sick. People still die. People still sin. There's evil in the world, and evil often appears triumphant.

Christians are caught in this very oxymoronic kind of situation, claiming on the one side the outrageous proposition that God has won, that humans are reconciled, that God has shared humanity, and that humans share in God's power proleptically. Yet, the world seems to continue to run on the same rails it has always run on.

What happens is that, for example, in I Corinthians 15, in Paul's letter to the Corinthians, he talks about the Resurrection of Jesus as the first fruits, using the term from Jewish sacrifice. The "first fruits" is like the first part of a harvest that represents the rest of the harvest. Thus, Jesus's Resurrection is the first fruits of the Resurrection of all that is going to happen in the future.

Christians then talk about the *parousia*, the Second Coming of Jesus, as the full realization of God's triumph, which will be empirically visible. Christians approach the 2,000-year-long story of the church from multiple perspectives. They agree on dividing Christian history into discreet segments that combine religious and secular dimensions; you have Apostolic period, the first two centuries; a Patristic period, third through the sixth centuries; the Medieval period, seventh through the 14th centuries; the Renaissance, 15th century and 16th century; the Reformation in the 16th century; the Enlightenment in the 17th century and 18th century; the Modern in the 19th century; and the Contemporary in the 20th and 21st centuries.

Christians have these rough-and-ready terms to use for those parts or segments of their story, yet the valuation of those segments is very, very different—depending on which group you belong to of Christianity. For people who belong to the Reformation—the Protestant tradition—the Patristic period and Medieval period are regarded as a great decline from original purity and original enthusiasm and of corruption.

From the other side, however, the Medieval period is regarded by many Roman Catholics as the greatest period of the church's flourishing, and the Reformation, until very recently, had been regarded as a pretty tragic mistake. They thought it not only disunified Christianity, but also led to severe errors in understanding Christianity.

For all Christians today, as I will show in our final lecture, the impact of the Enlightenment, or what we call modernity, more severely divides Christians perhaps than any other phenomenon in its long story.

Finally, Christians share the conviction that their story has a goal. The English literary critic Frank Kermode has written a wonderful book on eschatology called *The Sense of an Ending*. He uses the image of Christians as people who have had one shoe drop and are waiting for the other shoe to drop. They've heard the tick, but they're waiting for the tock. Christianity has this sense of a goal, but there is within Christianity much less agreement about what that goal looks like. The notion of an "age to come," or a "world to come," has fluctuated in importance in different periods in Christian history. Already in the late second century, a group called the Montanists fully expected Jesus to return and to establish the new Jerusalem in the small town of Pepuza in ancient Phrygia. The prophet Montanus and his helper Priscilla predicted that this was going to happen shortly.

Throughout the history of Christianity there have been powerful millenarian movements. The term *millenarian* comes from the term "millennium," which is the expectation of a thousand-year reign of God on earth, which is predicted in the Book of Revelation, chapter 21. In different periods, especially when centuries turn, there have been powerful millenarian movements within Christianity, people whose entire focus is future.

Today, especially in North America and in Latin America, Millenarian Christianity is one of the most rapidly growing movements. This is a very powerful movement within Christianity today. We find an example of it, for example, in David Koresh and the Branch Davidians at Waco in recent decades, the sort of reading of the contemporary story in terms of the Book of Revelation, and the expectation that the end time is coming soon.

Many, many Christians disagree with that view of the future completely. They hold a much more evolutionary view of Christian development and of the future. For example, a movement called the Social Gospel, and more recently Liberation Theology, within Christianity, has seen the future not as cataclysmic—not as an in-breaking by God, which is going to result in a rapture, carrying away f souls, Armageddon, and the destruction of the created world in a great fireball—but rather in terms of the battle in which God joins through Christ against oppressive social structures. Liberation Theology, in particular, has seen the future in terms of the possibilities for humanity that can be realized first within the church.

What Christians Believe
Lecture 5

Today, we consider the creed, what Christians believe. ... In contrast to many religions, belief or doctrine holds a disproportionately important part in Christianity.

Belief, or doctrine, occupies an unusually central place in Christianity, compared to other religious traditions. Some religions, including Judaism and Islam, place more emphasis on *orthopraxy* ("right practice") than on *orthodoxy* ("right opinion"). The Christian emphasis on belief is connected to its origins and early development. Its beginnings as a Jewish sect required making a choice for Jesus as Messiah and Lord. The experience of Jesus among followers gave rise to diverse understandings, requiring ever more elaborate statements of belief as a means of self-definition.

Christian belief is expressed formally by creeds and doctrines that have developed over time in response to internal conflict. The rudimentary statements of belief in the New Testament developed into the Apostles' Creed. The standard expression of faith for most Christians is the Nicene-Constantinopolitan Creed (325–381). Although all Christians emphasize belief, no single creed commands the assent of all Christians. Some groups have developed creedal statements that reflect their particular perspectives (see the Westminster Confession). Other groups reject the classic creeds but nevertheless retain certain convictions as a lens for reading Scripture.

Although Christianity is correctly called a monotheistic religion, its understanding of a triune God is complex. As in Judaism and Islam, "God" is considered first as the all-powerful creator of all things "visible and invisible" and, as the source of all reality, is termed "Father." But Christians also confess as God "the Son," who shares fully in the divine life and power. This son entered human history as Jesus Christ, the savior. Finally, the "Holy Spirit" is equally God, "worshipped and glorified with the Father and the Son." Christians consider that the way God is revealed through creation, salvation, and sanctification truly discloses the inner life of God as "three persons in one nature."

After centuries of debate concerning the work and nature of Jesus, Christians came to an equally complex understanding of Christology. The New Testament ascribes both divine and human attributes to Jesus, and both have been considered essential to the full appreciation of the savior. A heresy called *Monophysitism* so emphasized the divinity of Jesus that it virtually suppressed his humanity. Another heresy called *Nestorianism* emphasized Jesus's humanity to the extent that his divine nature seemed neglected. The Council of Chalcedon (451) declared that the orthodox understanding of Jesus must recognize that he is "two natures in one person"; that is, he is "true God and true man." Because the orthodox position is also profoundly paradoxical, Christian practice and piety have tended to focus either on the humanity or on the divinity of Jesus.

The creed leaves relatively undeveloped the nature and work of the Holy Spirit,

The creed leaves relatively undeveloped the nature and work of the Holy Spirit, and the appreciation for the Holy Spirit varies among Christian groups. The Holy Spirit "speaks through the prophets" and is active in God's self-revelation to humans. The Holy Spirit is active also in the process of human transformation that Christians call "sanctification."

The creed contains other affirmations that provide a frame for Christian identity and the basis for a coherent view of the world:

- Creation is good in all its aspects, but "sin" is a disordered use of the world by humans.

- Humans will be judged on the basis of their deeds.

- The church is a community that seeks to be one, holy, catholic, and apostolic.

- The present age prepares for God's final triumph in "the world to come." ■

Essential Reading

J. H. Leith, *Creeds of the Churches: A Reader in Christian Doctrine from the Bible to the Present* (Atlanta: John Knox Press, 1982).

Supplemental Reading

L.T. Johnson, *The Creed: What Christians Believe and Why It Matters* (New York: Doubleday, 2003).

J. N. D. Kelly, *Early Christian Doctrines*, revised edition (San Francisco: Harper and Row, 1960).

Questions to Consider

1. Why is "right belief" so critical to Christianity, in contrast to other religions?

2. Is Christianity "monotheistic" in the same sense that Judaism and Islam are monotheistic?

3. Comment on this proposition: "The Christian view of the world is more optimistic than pessimistic, and the Christian drama is more comedy than tragedy."

What Christians Believe
Lecture 5—Transcript

In our last presentation, we saw that one of the things that holds Christians together and gives them a sense of identity is that they share a long story, a story which gives them a sense of place in the world and a sense of participation in the world's destiny. It is a simple story of a fall from favor with God, a restoration to favor with God through the work of Jesus Christ, and a hope of full participation in God's life in a future life.

This story is drawn from Scripture—from the experience and the history of the community. It provides an interpretation of the world and it answers those three great existential questions that all humans are faced with. Where do we come from? Christians answer, "We come from a loving and creating God." Who are we? Christians answer, "We are God's children who have been saved through the sacrifice of Jesus Christ." Where are we going? Christians say, "We hope we're going to share more fully in God's life in a future resurrection."

This brings us in the present presentation to a second element that binds many Christians together, and that is their belief or doctrine. Today, we consider the creed, what Christians believe. Here we see another way in which religion is not simply about experience, but also about conviction.

In contrast to many religions, belief or doctrine holds a disproportionately important part in Christianity. In fact, this is one of the ways in which Christians often misconstrue other religious traditions because belief—"What do we profess? What do we think? What are our convictions?"—is so important to Christians that they assume that it is important to all other religions as well. Thus, they turn to other religious traditions and they ask, "What do you believe?" when in fact other religious traditions would want to respond in terms of, "What is it that I'm doing? What are our practices?"

Take, for example, the two other great Western traditions. In Judaism the emphasis is entirely upon keeping the commandments of God, the *Mitzvoth*, and being an observant Jew. Judaism has managed to survive for millennia with the simple proclamation that is found in the Book of Deuteronomy, the *Shma Yisrael*. "Here, Oh Israel, the Lord your God is one, and you shall put no other God before this God, but you shall love the Lord your God with all your heart and all your might and all your soul." When Moses Mimonades introduced the more elaborate frame of creed in the 12th century, many Jews resisted this, and it has never become a kind of normative part of Judaism.

Similarly, for Muslims to be *Islama,* to be submissive, is to do the Five Pillars of Islam. It is not an elaborate set of beliefs that define a Muslim. One of those pillars, to be sure, is the *Shahadah*, which is the simple declaration, "I proclaim" or "I confess that *Allah* alone is God and Muhammad is his *Rasul,*" his prophet or ambassador. Beyond that, however, Islam has no need for a further elaboration of a creed.

Why, then, is belief so important in Christianity? It has to do with how Christianity originated out of its kind of experience, and its early development. Jesus himself, as the Gospels show, undoubtedly shared the simple profession of faith of Israel that God is one, and we see in early Christian writers—Paul and James—the same profession, God is one.

If Jesus is proclaimed as Messiah, though, that Jesus is Christ, that begins to introduce not only a positive assertion, but—by implication—a negative one. If Jesus is Messiah, then others are not messiahs. There's a way of sort of defining Christianity within Judaism, making a choice, a plus but also a minus.

Even more dramatically, to say that Jesus is Lord because of the experience of the Resurrection, means that one's understanding of the oneness of God now becomes more complicated. What does it mean to say that God is Lord? Remember that that's the very name of God in the Hebrew bible, *Yahweh* or *Kyrios*, and also to say that Jesus is Lord.

We see this complication already within 24 years of Jesus's death, when Paul is writing to the Corinthian church. He says in chapter 8, verses 4-6, "We know that no idol in the world really exists," speaking as a good Jew here, "and that there is no God but one. Indeed, even though there may be many so-called Gods in heaven or on earth," in fact there are many gods and many lords, the Gentile religions, "yet for us there is one God, the Father, from whom are all things, and for whom we exist."

This is a perfectly Jewish profession of faith. In contrast to all the pretend gods of the pagans, the idols, there is but one God who is the father and the source of all reality. Now Paul complicates it: "And one Lord, Jesus Christ, through whom are all things and through whom we exist." The experience of Jesus as resurrected Lord, and as sharing the full life of God, complicates the Christian understanding of the oneness of God. This is not after centuries of development. It's there really in the experience itself, from the beginning.

We also see that the experience of Jesus as Lord gave rise to diverse understandings from the beginning. Already, in the New Testament, we see that there were some in Johannine Christianity addressed in the first and second letters of John, who were denying the full humanity of Jesus. They were denying that Jesus Christ came in the flesh, John said, and they were being pushed out of the community because their understanding of Jesus was not the proper understanding.

Similarly, I suggested in an earlier presentation that in the second century that movement called Gnosticism offered a Christ who was not really human, but only appeared as human. This is called *docetism*, from the Greek word "to appear." God did not take on full humanity, but only sort of rode a body through history, and therefore he only appeared in human form.

These kinds of differences of interpretation increasingly put pressure on the Christian community to develop its understanding of the experience. The difficulty in Christian history is that sometimes the understanding has tended to replace the experience. The understanding or the articulation to express in words has always been intended as a way of protecting the character of the experience, not to replace the experience.

We begin to see the development of Christian belief first in the liturgy, in the ritual of baptism. In the early second century, we see that when somebody offered himself or herself to the church to be baptized, to be initiated into the community, that the ritual transition from unbelief to belief was marked, of course, by being plunged into water and coming out of water. Before that plunging, there was a question and answer format of "Do you believe? Do you believe?" by which the person to be baptized certified, indeed, that she/he did share the convictions of this community that she/he was now joining.

By the middle of the second century, we see that this kind of statement of belief had developed into a creed-al formula that is called the Apostles' Creed. This is a form of belief that is contemporarily shared by many Christians. Catholics pray this creed at the beginning of that devotional called the Rosary. Many Protestants use this creed in their Sunday worship. It goes like this. "I believe in God, the Father Almighty, creator of heaven and earth, and in Jesus Christ, his only son, our Lord, who was conceived by the Holy Spirit, born of the Virgin Mary, suffered under Pontius Pilate, was crucified, died, and buried. He descended into hell. On the third day, he rose again from the dead, ascended to heaven, and sits on the right hand of God, the Father Almighty. Thence he will come to judge the living and the dead. I believe in the Holy Spirit, the Holy Catholic church, the communion of saints, the forgiveness of sins, the resurrection of the body and life everlasting."

If you look carefully at this creed, you will see that it is dominated by the story of Jesus. It is fundamentally a basic statement about God as creator, a basic statement about the Holy Spirit and the church, but fundamentally the creed gives an epitome of the Christian story, of that part of the story by which Jesus was God incarnate, died for humans, and then went back to share the life of God.

In the course of time over the next couple of centuries, challenges to this understanding continued to be raised. And, in particular, an Alexandrian priest by the name of Arius in the beginning of the fourth century challenged for the first time (really) in Christianity the divinity of Jesus—not his humanity, but his divinity. He was convinced that since God is one, then anything other than God, the Father, must be a creature. Therefore, the Son must be a creature. Therefore, Jesus is not really God, but a kind of courtesan-queen, a kind of half god-half man, kind of amalgam.

In response to the Arian controversy, one of the first things that the Emperor Constantine did when Christianity became the religion of the Empire, was to call the orthodox bishops together in the Council of Nicea in 325. They developed a more elaborate form of the creed. Since that didn't completely end the controversy, in 381 another council was called at the city of Constantinople, and as a result there came about the Nicene-Constantinopolitan Creed, a difficult thing to pronounce, which is the creed that is used today by the Catholic and Orthodox traditions in their liturgy.

It reads in this fashion: "We believe in one God, the Father Almighty, creator or maker of heaven and earth of all things, visible and invisible, and in one Lord Jesus Christ, the only begotten Son of God, begotten from the Father before all ages, light from light, true God from true God, begotten, not created, of the same essence of the Father, through whom all things came into being, who for us men and for our salvation came down from heaven, and was incarnate by the Holy Spirit and the Virgin Mary, and became man. He was crucified for us under Pontius Pilate, suffered, died, and was buried. On the third day, according to the Scriptures, he ascended into heaven and sits on the right hand of the Father. He will come again in glory to judge the living and the dead, and of his kingdom there will be no end. We believe in the Holy Spirit, the Lord and giver of life who proceeds from the Father, who is worshipped and glorified together with the Father and the Son who spoke through the prophets, and in one Holy Catholic and Apostolic church, we confess one baptism for the forgiveness of sins. We look forward to the resurrection of the dead and the life of the world to come. Amen."

You will notice that this is a much more elaborate creed than the Apostles' Creed. We have to develop the notion that "God" is creator of all things, both "visible and invisible." Why? Because of Marcionism, that denied that God could have anything to do with material reality. God is the source, not only of spiritual things, but of material things. Most of all, we find expanded that part dealing with the Son before he becomes human. He really is God. He is not a creature.

Most Christians share this basic statement of belief. Some Christians do not. They are fundamentally against creeds in general. These are particularly

Evangelical Christians, Christians who belong to Free Church traditions like Baptists, who think that creeds are too constraining on the freedom of Christians, and so they do not adhere to these standard professions of belief. Even those who say our only authority is the Bible, such as fundamentalists, nevertheless have convictions in light of which they read the Bible. That's why they are fundamentalists. There are certain fundamental convictions that they find in the Bible, such as the Bible is inerrant, such as Jesus is divine, such as Jesus was born of a virgin birth. Even fundamentalists who reject these explicit creeds have a framework of conviction and belief that guides their reading of Scripture.

What I would like to do now is review the basic structure of Christian belief and touch upon some of the important elements in this belief. Begin with the most obvious: Although Christianity is called a monotheistic religion, its understanding of God is far more complex than the other monotheistic traditions. For Christianity, the oneness of God is not singularity, but unity. Christians believe in a Triune God, three persons in one God, usually called the Trinity.

As in Judaism and Islam, "God," the term *Theos* in Greek, is considered first as the all powerful creator of everything, all things visible and invisible—because God is the source of all reality and is designated by the term "Father." "Our Father" is the characteristic Christian prayer. Jesus calls God "My Father."

Christians also confess, as God, "the Son," who shares fully in the divine life and power. What makes this very complicated is that, as I said earlier, the Christian experience of the Resurrection of Jesus had them read back the divinity of Jesus into his ministry and even before. We see this already in Paul; he says "we have one Lord Jesus Christ, through whom are all things." This Son is, as Christians term it, preexistent, shares God's life even before becoming human. The Son partakes in creation, and it is this Son then that enters humanity in Jesus, and partakes of humanity, and saves humanity by elevating it beyond its previous condition.

Finally, "Holy Spirit" is the third designation that Christians give to God, who, the creed says, is to be "worshipped and glorified with the Father and the Son." What's going on here? What's going on is that Christians are trying to express, with prepositional language, a very inadequate term the complex way, in which Christians have experienced the divine in their lives. That experience is creation, salvation, and sanctification—this power that is at work in them. They are convinced that the way in which God has disclosed God's self in the experience of humanity through creation, through salvation in Jesus Christ, through this power that has been released in humans called the Holy Spirit, that that process of revelation is really revelation. It really discloses who God is in God's inner life. If God has revealed God's self in three *prosopa (prosopon)*; the Greek word is not really our word, person—like an individual, but really rather a "mask," or an "appearance," a "presentation." If God has appeared to us in three distinct presentations, then that also reveals God's inner life.

The Christian understanding of God is that of the Trinity, as of "three persons who share one nature," so that whatever the father is, that is also the Son. Whatever worship and glory you give to the Son and the Father, you give also to the Spirit. The inner life of God is a community life, an inner life of giving of being, and receiving of being in almost a kind of eternal dance. In fact, the term used in Greek theology for this is *perichoresis*, which is a kind of divine dance that describes the inner life of God.

After centuries of debate within Christianity, especially as Christianity became more philosophically sophisticated, and tried harder and harder to express its experiences in the form of convictions and propositions, debate over the work and nature of Jesus yielded an equally complex understanding of Christology. The term "Christology" means the understanding or the study of the Christ, the Messiah.

Although the New Testament itself rarely uses the title *Theos*, God, for Jesus, it does so about three or four times. It usually reserves that title for God the Father. Nevertheless, the New Testament does ascribe to Jesus both human and divine attributes, and this is the case in all of the New

Testament writings, not simply the Gospels, but also the letters, the earliest Christian writings.

Thus, on one side, Jesus is fully and manifestly human. He is born. He experiences fatigue. He has relationships with other humans. He grows weary. He suffers. He is executed. He really dies, and he is buried. He's planted, like all other humans. He's truly dead.

On the other side, however, attributes are ascribed to Jesus such as he is life-giver. He can transform nature, and his is the judge of humans. This combination of divine and human attributes yields a very complex image of who Jesus is, and Christians in the early centuries tended to tilt back and forth between two emphases.

On one side there was an overemphasis on his divinity, and this was a heresy called *Monophysitism*. The word means "one nature," which really, much like Gnosticism, envisaged Jesus as so much divine even in his human appearance that it was almost as though God simply took hold of a body and directed it through a human lifetime.

On the other extreme, often in a form of a heresy called *Nestorianism* from the teacher Nestorius, the humanity was so emphasized that again, Jesus's divinity tended to be minimized.

Therefore, the Council of Ephesus, in the year 431, convened to consider this matter. The Christian monks rioted in the streets chanting the phrase, "Theotocos, Theotocos," which means "mother of God, mother of God," because what the Nestorians were denying was that Mary could appropriately be called the mother of God, since she was patently the mother of a human being, you see. The Orthodox party insisted that it is appropriate to call Mary the mother of God, as indeed Christians do to this day.

These tensions, emphasis on the humanity and Nestorianism, emphasis on the divinity and Monophysitism, riots in the streets, theology can be exciting, led finally to the Council of Chalcedon in the year 451. It depended very heavily on the theological work of the bishop of Rome, Leo I, usually called

Leo the Great, and declared the position of the church with regard to Jesus. This is standard for Christians today; that is to say that in Jesus Christ we have "two natures in one person." Notice the use of philosophical language, two fusing in one person, *prosopon*. He is both God and man.

The church basically said, "Here's the playing field. You have to assert that Jesus is both divine and human and fully both; if you try to solve the puzzle of how he can be both, you're going to tilt the balance in one way or the other."

Therefore, fundamentally, the Christian position on Christology is that they'd rather have the mystery, which preserves the experience, than have conceptual clarity. They would rather deal with paradox than with a solution that diminishes the experience. Since that Orthodox position is so profoundly paradoxical, Christian practice and Christian piety frequently focus either on the humanity or on the divinity of Jesus, because it is extraordinarily hard, perhaps impossible, to focus on both at once.

Therefore, you have forms of piety in which Jesus is supremely God, the divine, the second person in the Trinity, the one who saves us, who rescues us, who guides us. In another form of piety, Jesus is the human who can be imitated in his human life.

I want to emphasize, however, that often both forms of piety can be found in the same community and in the same person at different moments, so that at one moment a person can emphasize the humanity of Jesus, at another his divinity. This is a very complex form of belief.

The creed leaves relatively undeveloped the work and the person of the Holy Spirit. The New Testament evidence on the Holy Spirit is equally ambiguous and complex. On one side, the Holy Spirit tends to be described as a power, almost as an energy field that possesses, occupies, drives, inspires, and enables Christians to do things.

On the other side, New Testament texts speak of the spirit as willing, deciding, choosing, selecting, and discerning. These are all attributes of persons. Persons will decide, choose, select, discern. Thus, out of this ambiguous language about the spirit, yes, a power, but also, yes, personal, there is the development of the teaching about the Holy Spirit in the creed. The Holy Spirit "speaks through the prophets" and is active in God's self-revelation to humans. Christianity in this sense is a prophetic religion. It is convinced that God, through the Holy Spirit, spoke through the prophets of old, like Isaiah and Amos, through Jesus who is a prophet, and continues to speak through prophets in the church.

The Holy Spirit is also active in the process that Christians call "sanctification"—that is it is the Holy Spirit that transforms them into the image of Jesus. Paul talks about this in his second letter to the Corinthians, chapter 3, verses 17-18, where he says, "Now the Lord is the spirit, and where the spirit of the Lord is, there is freedom, and all of us with unveiled faces see the glory of the Lord as though reflected in a mirror, and are being transformed into the same image from one degree of glory to another, for this comes from the Lord, the spirit." The Holy Spirit is the agent or the means of transformation of humans into the image of Jesus, the humanity of Jesus. As Paul says in Romans 8, Jesus can be the first born of many brothers. Jesus is like the elder brother of those who are shaped into his image.

For Christians throughout the world today, the Holy Spirit's importance varies considerably. For some Christians, the Holy Spirit is simply a rather odd way of designating God, one of the persons of the Trinity, something of an afterthought. There are forms of Christianity, though, and they are powerful and growing forms of Christianity, for whom the work of the Holy Spirit is the entire point. They are very much based in the experience of the Holy Spirit. These are called "Charismatic Christians." The word "charisma" refers in Greek to the gifts of the Holy Spirit, such as prophecy and speaking in tongues, or Pentecostal Christians. The term "Pentecost" comes from the Jewish feast 50 days after Passover, which, according to the Acts of the Apostles, was the day on which the Holy Spirit was poured out on the first Christians. Consequently, Pentecostal or Charismatic Christians have a deep devotion to the spirit and see the activity of the Holy Spirit in people's lives as being the authentic verification of really being a Christian.

The creed provides other affirmations that establish a kind of frame for Christian identity and the basis for a coherent view of the world. Creation is good in all of its aspects. Humans are created in the image of God and are created free, yet they misuse that freedom in what is called "sin," and thereby distort creation and need to be rescued by God's favor and God's empowerment, in order to do the things pleasing to God. The church is a community of people who have been touched by this Holy Spirit, and it has as its ideals unity, holiness, inclusiveness, catholicity, and apostolicity, which means a connection with the earliest Church of the Apostles and a faithfulness to the ideals of the earliest church.

Baptism is the ritual of initiation is for the forgiveness of sins, which means that a person who is being baptized is forgiven the sins that they have committed; she or he also joins a community, which is one that is committed to the forgiveness of sins, and to reconciliation, and to the expression of compassion.

Finally, Christians belong to a community that prepares and anticipates God's rule over the world, and over all reality in the age to come.

The Christian creed provides a guide for reading Scripture, a set of boundaries for the Christian community, and a coherent interpretation of the world. In the liturgy, as Christians profess these beliefs, they move from the role of participants and auditors of the word of God, and the readings of Scripture and the prayers, to the participation in the Lord's Supper, the meal by which they join in the celebration of the power and the presence of the risen Lord.

The Church and Sacraments
Lecture 6

The most dramatic and unexpected development in Christianity happened by accident, though at the time it appeared to be divine providence.

The conflict with Gnosticism had defined Christianity as an embodied and institutional religion, but the establishment of Christianity as the imperial religion had a profound effect on its public presence. Its status shifted from that of a persecuted minority to a state-sponsored majority; fervor was no longer a requirement of membership. It changed overnight from a group that met secretly in households and catacombs to an organization in charge of basilicas and public charities. Although the local congregation was still of fundamental importance, an elaborate superstructure of administration for the church matched that of the empire.

Although from its earliest days Christianity had forms of structure drawn from Greco-Roman and Jewish antecedents, its growth and public involvement led to elaborate patterns of hierarchy. Even before Constantine, the simple administrative structure reflected in the Pauline letters had become more hierarchical. A single bishop (*episcopos*) emerged as head over a board of elders (*presbyteroi*) and deacons (*diakonoi*). This arrangement was legitimated in terms of cultic language (priesthood/sacrifice). Christianity thenceforth consisted of two great classes: the clergy and the laity. Under empire, hierarchical structures became even more elaborate, both at the local level (orders of clergy leading to priesthood and episcopacy) and at the regional level (patriarchs). The patriarch of the imperial city (Rome, then Constantinople) asserted authority over the entire "ecumenical" church.

With the expansion of the church's structure and its occupation of great public spaces for worship its own liturgy (public worship) also became more elaborate. In the few glimpses of early Christian worship given by the New Testament, baptism and the Lord's Supper emerge as two ritual activities, centered in the experience of the death and resurrection of Jesus. In the imperial period, both expand in dramatic ways as liturgy grows to fill the space allotted to it. The basilicas have a fundamental structure of a long hallway, called a *nave*, at the end of which is usually a circular space called the *apse*. In the apse is the sanctuary, where the ritual activity is centered.

The later Gothic cathedrals have a *transept*, a horizontal expansion in the nave, so that the church takes on the form of the cross. In this large space, the clergy and priests carry out the activities of worship, while members of the congregation

Christianity reached into every aspect of life, finding ways of sanctifying time and space.

become observers. The clergy take on vestments, processions, music, incense, and bells, the accoutrements of a public event. Baptism becomes an elaborate and public ritual of initiation at the Easter Vigil that is preceded by months of preparation. The Eucharist (Mass), as celebrated by a bishop in a basilica, loses much of its quality as a meal and gains a quality of public, even civic, ceremony.

Christianity reached into every aspect of life, finding ways of sanctifying time and space. The sanctification of time was both communal and individual. The sacraments of the church grew beyond baptism and the Eucharist to include confirmation, matrimony, holy orders, penance, and the anointing of the sick. The "liturgical year" sanctified time through the celebration of the events of Jesus's life, death, and resurrection in two great cycles: the Easter cycle and the Christmas cycle. Martyrs and confessors were considered as "saints" whose lives revealed the power of the divine in Christ and were exemplary and efficacious for other believers.

The sanctification of space developed later but reflected the same impulse to bring everything into the realm of the sacred. Pilgrimage to "holy places" (especially the Holy Land) begins in the 4th century and grows in popularity. Reverence for the tombs of the martyrs grows into the cult of relics, which extends their influence through space and time. ■

Essential Reading

B. Thompson, *Liturgies of the Western Church* (Philadelphia: Fortress Press, 1961).

Supplemental Reading

D. Bloesch, *The Church: Sacraments, Worship, Ministry, Mission* (Christian Foundations; Downers Grove, IL: InterVarsity Press, 2002).

G. Dix, *The Shape of the Liturgy*, 2nd edition (New York: Seabury Press, 1982).

J. Macquarrie, *A Guide to the Sacraments* (New York: Continuum, 1997).

Questions to Consider

1. What complexities entered into Christianity as a result of its steady growth in numbers and its adaptation as the imperial religion?

2. Discuss the concept of *sanctification* as it is manifested in sacraments, saints, and sacred sites.

3. How does the liturgical year create an alternative world to that of secular time and activity?

The Church and Sacraments
Lecture 6—Transcript

Religion, including Christianity, is not just belief. It's about practice. It's not just what people think or profess; it has to do with what people do, and what people do together.

In the next several lectures, we will be considering Christian practice. As I mentioned in the last presentation, many Christians think of their religion in terms of belief, and tend to look at other religions in terms of their beliefs. In fact, however, practice is extremely important in Christianity.

In this class, we'll talk about the church and the sacraments and worship. In the next class, we'll talk about morality. Then, we'll talk about the radical edge in Christianity in terms of practice.

The most dramatic and unexpected development in Christianity happened by accident, though at the time it appeared to be divine providence; that was the decision by Constantine in the year 313—not only to tolerate Christianity, which formerly had been persecuted, but even to make it the established religion of the Empire. Later, I will consider the political implications of this dramatic decision. Now, though, I want to look at the profound effect this change had on Christian practice, especially the organization of the church and its worshipping.

The conflict with Gnosticism in the second century, we saw, had already defined Christianity as an embodied and institutional religion. In contrast to Gnosticism's preference for the purely spiritual, Christianity said, "No, bodies are important." In contrast to Gnosticism's preference for the individual, Christianity said, "No, we need a visible organization. We need a structure. We are a people, a community."

The establishment of Christianity as the imperial religion had a profound effect on its public presence. Its status shifted from that of a persecuted minority, the age of the martyrs, remember, to a state-sponsored majority.

Obviously, fervor was no longer a requirement for membership. Christianity was in a privileged position, and membership had its rewards.

Christianity changed overnight, and virtually with no preparation, from a group that met quietly and perhaps even clandestinely in private households, and even in the catacombs, burial places in various cities, to an organization that was visible, public, and was given by Constantine great public buildings, the basilicas, which were originally halls of justice, to use for their worship.

They were given a hand in the various public charities—running orphanages, running hospitals, running the welfare system of the city and the state. This had a tremendous impact on how Christianity began to emerge. Although under Constantine, the local congregation, the *ekklesia*, as local congregation, still was important, an elaborate superstructure of administration for the church began increasingly to match, even mimic, the bureaucracy of the Empire.

Let's look first, then, at these forms of organization. From its earliest days, Christianity had a formal structure that was largely drawn from Greco-Roman clubs and schools on one side, and the Jewish synagogue on the other side, namely a simple structure of a board of administrators, called the *gerousia*, or *presbyteroi*; a board of elders, with a revolving office called the superintendent, the *episcopos*; the bishop; and some subordinate roles filled by people who were basically called helpers—men and women who were diaconal and did the practical chores.

The growth of Christianity numerically, and above all its public posture now under Constantine, began to develop a more elaborate form of what is called "hierarchy."

The term "hierarchy," of course, means "holy power," and is a regimented form of power by which holiness is mediated from the top to the bottom.

Even before Constantine, we begin to see the emergence of some signs of this moving from the simple structure reflected in the Pauline letters to people like Ignatius and Polycarp, whom we mentioned in an earlier presentation;

they thought of a single *episcopos* as a sort of monarch within each community, as being over the board of elders and the deacons. Increasingly, this arrangement was legitimated by theological language. It was legitimated in terms of using the language of priesthood, borrowed from the Jewish cult, and the language of sacrifice, so that the administration of the church shifted over the course of centuries from a simple practical arrangement to get things done, increasingly to an order of clergy who were distinct from the laity.

Consequently, we now have a professional class within Christianity called the clergy, who were more educated, more trained, and devoted themselves entirely to the work of the church, and the laity. The word "lay," means of course, the non-professional; she or he also therefore tended to be less educated, non-specialized in his or her work, and very often supported the clergy financially as well.

Under the Empire, hierarchical structures became ever more elaborate, both at the local level—so that in a local level of the church you would have a bishop presiding over the church, but then you would have priests beneath the bishop, and deacons below them, so three orders of clergy, but then increasingly ever more elaborate steps leading up to the priesthood. Functions within the community that formerly may have been carried out by different people, readers, exorcists, and so forth, now became stages toward elevation. Now one went from being an acolyte; to a lector; to a thurifer, somebody who carried the smoke; to exorcist; to sub-deacon; to deacon; to priesthood. You begin to get a very elaborate internal structure of organization. That's at the local level.

Then at the regional level, you had patriarchs, father rulers, who would be the main bishop—often the term used is "archbishop," a ruling bishop, over a larger area. And even above that, the empyreal city and the bishop at the empyreal city. First Rome, and then Constantinople, tended to become the patriarchs with the most punch. The bishop of Rome and the bishop of Constantinople were, therefore, administrative leaders for vast geographical areas. The church became not so much a local organism, as a very complex organization, increasingly, in this period. That, of course, has a number of implications, none of which I'm going to go into at this moment, but will pick up in later presentations.

I want to turn to the notion of worship. With the expansion of the church's structures, and its occupation of these great public spaces for its worship, its own liturgy, or public worship, also became more elaborate. Notice that the very word "liturgy" is used in ancient Greece for the public works of city-states; that is, the festivals, the processions, the feasts in celebration of various gods. Wealthy patrons would put up the money to enable these public works to be done for the religious and civic good of the community. Christian worship now, interestingly, comes to be called liturgy, a great public work. Again, we move in the direction of complication.

Our few glimpses of early Christian worship in the New Testament, such as baptism and the Lord's Supper, emerge as fairly simple ritual activities, centered in the experience of the death and Resurrection of Jesus. Baptism was a simple ritual of initiation, in which a person, as we saw in the last presentation, professed their commitment to Christian belief, took off his or her clothing, plunged into water, came out of the water, was given new white garments and a candle to hold, and then would enter into a sharing of the Lord's Supper. The Lord's Supper was basically a simple meal, a shared meal of bread and wine, sometimes also bread and water in some communities, or bread and fish in some communities, but basically a meal that was an expression of fellowship among the believers, but a fellowship that was based in a deeper spiritual fellowship, the resurrected Jesus.

Already in the year 54, Paul talks about participating in the body and blood of Jesus when they ate meals together, so that there's a strong sense that this is not an ordinary meal, but is a meal which gives a participation in the life and death of Jesus, and an anticipation of Jesus's second coming. It was not ordinary, but it was simple, and it was communal, and it was genuinely a meal. You could gather around a card table and have Christian worship, you see.

What happens when this card table in the cave is transported to the great basilicas of Rome, the great halls of justice?

What happens is that worship needs to expand to fill the space allotted to it. The basilicas, therefore, have a fundamental structure of a very long hallway called the *nave*, often with aisles on the side, but it goes on and on. The word *nave* comes from the word "ship" (*naves*,) so you have that sense of this long interior, and at the end of it is often a circular space called the *apse*.

In the *apse* is the sanctuary, which is the holy place. That's where the ritual activity tends to take place. Later, in particular, in gothic cathedrals, which developed in the Middle Ages, there is also a *transept*, which, as the word suggests, is a horizontal expansion in the *nave*, so that if you would look at a Christian cathedral from the sky you would see it in the form of a cross, with the *nave* leading to the *apse*, and then the *transept* cutting across it. This is a very large space. What would this suggest about worship?

The sanctuary is going to be the place where the professionals are, the clergy, the priests who carry out the worship in the holy place. Where are the other participants?

They are the laity. They are going to be in the position less of participants and more as observers of activity that is being carried out by professionals. Because there are these larger spaces, you can't put a card table at the end of the great basilica and have a homey meal. One needs to be representative of the grandeur of Rome. What happens is that the clergy now take on the vestments, the ornate garb of priests. You have processions, movement, you have music to accompany these long spaces, you have lots of smoke, indicating a divine service is in process, you have bells, you have whistles. In other words, all of the things that are accoutrements of a public event now become ingredient to Christian worship. This is a simple function of change of place, going from a table in a household, or a card table in a cave, to occupying a huge public space and needing to represent, in some sense, the empyreal religion.

Thus, in terms of organizational complexity, and in terms of architecture, and in terms of the worship that takes place in that architecture, we are seeing Christianity, in the blink of an eye, move from the simple, the persecuted, the minority, to a majority and public posture in which most Christians now become observers of a professional class who are the real Christians, the clergy, the ministers. This is a dramatic change in the Christian religion.

Let's just revisit baptism and the Eucharist. Baptism now becomes an elaborate process and ritual of initiation, which is celebrated not when you want to become a Christian, and we dunk you in water and accept you into the community, but it becomes a large formal event celebrated once a year at the Easter Vigil, Easter being the celebration of the death and Resurrection of Jesus on a set date, and it is preceded by a 40-day period of preparation of those called catechumens, those who are being instructed; they are given elaborate instructions in creed, in belief, in how to pray, and so forth and so on. Then, they are baptized in an all-night ceremony before the whole throng of the faithful. Baptism shifts its very shape because of these changes.

What about the Lord's Supper? It is now called the Eucharist, a Greek word that means "thanksgiving," or the Mass, and it also becomes something quite different than a meal shared around a table. It moves in the direction of a sacrificial drama. I mean, after all, the basilicas resembled Greek temples.

There you have the sanctuary, the holy place, you have the altar, you have the pulpit from which the word of God is proclaimed, so that one is not sharing in a meal so much as one is observing—in effect, a transmutation of ordinary elements, bread and wine, into the body and blood of the Lord. The point of the worship becomes less sharing in the meal; indeed, it's going to become a considerable problem later in Christianity, where people in fact avoid sharing in communion, that is the body and the blood, out of a sense of unworthiness because it is so holy; it is, after all, a divine element.

This means that in the Middle Ages, in the cathedrals, the high point of worship is not receiving the food into oneself and thereby sharing in a meal with fellow believers; the high point of the meal is showing the bread. At the showing of the bread, everybody reverences, and there is this sense of divine epiphany that takes place in that ceremony. The meal aspect tends to be lost almost completely. It's only in very recent years, in the last couple of hundred years, that that meal dimension has been restored within Christianity—in

Roman Catholicism, and not until the last 40 years. It is a tremendous change that takes place.

Of course, on high holy days, the solemn feasts, and I'll talk about those in a moment, liturgies could tend to become extraordinarily elaborate with all of these processions, long readings, chants, antiphons, and canticles. Time and space need to be filled. If you're a significant religion you need to worship significantly. Worship becomes something that is physically demanding and extremely impressive. Consequently, the Eucharist is even less a meal and more of a political and civic statement made by the Christian empire, if you like.

As I mentioned several times already, for ordinary Christians, it meant that sense of full identification with the community is more passive. To be a real Christian, you need to become a clergy person, a minister, or some other professional.

The other side of this expansion of time and space is that Christianity, in its new public profile, was able to reach into every aspect of life, finding ways of sanctifying both time and space. The sanctification of time was both communal and individual.

Here we come to the topic of the sacraments. Ritual extends itself beyond baptism and the Eucharist, to cover virtually all of the moments of passage through life's way. There develop, eventually, seven sacraments. (There is the Eucharist.) There is baptism, the ritual of initiation; there is confirmation, which is in effect the replacement of circumcision. It's a puberty rite. It is an anointing of a young person to welcome them to Christian adulthood. There are holy orders, becoming a minister or ordination, which as we saw is itself very complex.

There is matrimony, or marriage, for those who were lay and who would marry; there was the sacrament of reconciliation or penance, for people who committed sins, after baptism, could be reconciled to the church and have their further sins forgiven through, again, an elaborate process, a very serious penance often, and public reconciliation with the community.

Finally, there was the anointing of the sick, or sometimes called extreme unction, which was a final farewell to those who were departing for the other life. All the important moments of life, from birth to death, were marked by these ritual actions that are called the sacraments. They make those passages holy, and not simply profane.

Time was also sanctified in other ways. For example, Christians began to develop a sense of the week, as had Jews, as consisting of a special holy day and then the ordinary days. If you're thinking semiotically of the relationship between clergy and laity, between sacred and profane, think Sunday and the rest of the week. Rather than the weekly Sabbath in Judaism, Christians celebrated on the first day of the week, Sunday. It is the pagan name for that day, and is celebrated every week as a commemoration of Jesus's Resurrection. What is celebrated every Sunday is the Resurrection.

Time has to be sanctified entirely, however. What begins to happen is that the entire year becomes the "liturgical year." All of time is structured by Christian convictions and by the Christian experience, so that you have two great feasts that organize the entire Christian year. The most important is Easter.

However, Easter now is preceded by 40 days of preparation called Lent, which is a time of penitence, a time of preparation, of discipline and so forth. In Islam, this is Ramadan, and then you move increasingly into the celebration, indeed almost the reliving of the last days of Jesus's life; Holy Week intensifies that. You begin to move day-by-day through Jesus's last days. There are the sacred *triduum*, the last three days, his Last Supper, his death, his burial, and finally Easter, the Easter Vigil. Time then, is structured not on profane days, or pagan feasts, but around the Christian calendar.

Similarly and later, there is Christmas, the celebration of the Incarnation. Again, there is a 30-day season of preparation and penitence called Advent—awaiting the coming—then Christmas itself, and then the Feast of Epiphany on January sixth; this completes another cycle.

The high holy days have their time of preparation, then ordinary time, which is much more profane. As the movement of Christian life and Christian sanctification becomes even more complicated, though, even those empty times begin to become studded with the celebration of particular "saints," people who have been sanctified. The Christian liturgical year has the two great feasts of Christmas and Easter, but then throughout the year, the celebration of saints' days, in commemoration of these special people.

We have to talk for a moment, what is a saint, because this is a very important concept in Christianity. In the earliest period when Paul is writing his letters, when he writes his letters to the saints who are in Corinth, he just means all believers. He simply means that everybody who belongs to this realm called the Holy Spirit. It's simply a designation that Christians use for themselves. There's the world and there are the saints. As Christianity developed, however, it became clear that some people, especially martyrs, people who witness to their profession to the point of death, people like Jesus himself, Paul, Ignatius, Polycarp, and many, many others, in them the Holy Spirit's work was, if you will, completed, finished. They were made holy through their deaths. They were regarded as, in a sense, a realization of what God's work was about; that the whole point of Christianity was to make saints. Therefore, when people showed in their life, first of all in the way they died, but then increasingly confessors, not people who died for the faith, but people who endured for the faith, and who lived out their life in a particularly holy and convincing fashion, were regarded as the individual triumph of God in human life. Thus, for Christianity, the saints represent the point of it all, the transformation of human life and human freedom. The saints' days enter into the celebration of liturgical year.

With this develops the notion of a communion, in a sense. Part of the Christian story, part of the Christian experience, is to be part of a family. The letter to the Hebrews talks about a cloud of witnesses, who in fact are bound together through this process of sanctification—those who are struggling here, and those who have already accomplished this.

This is why, in Christian piety, we have the development of patron saints. Almost as within Greco-Roman polytheism, where one would appeal to an individual god or goddess as its particular patron, so within Christianity one would turn to a particular person—such as Mary (Jesus's mother), Saint Ignatius, or Saint Polycarp—as a particular patron who would be of assistance in this same process of transformation.

Along with the sanctification of time—through worship, through the sacraments, through the liturgical year—there was also the sanctification of space, which follows from this. As I've suggested, this is found first of all in the architecture of the church itself, in which you have a space which is holy to be sure, but rather more profane, the *nave*, but then the *apse* or the sanctuary, the place where the *achtus*, the liturgical action, takes place, is more holy. Once churches begin to be built by Christians themselves, they even begin to show orientation; that is to point in the direction of another holy place, namely Jerusalem. You've got this spatial directedness, then, of Christian architecture.

Already in the fourth century, we see the development of pilgrimage, that is the notion that it might be important to go to a place other than one's own, which is holier than one's own, and therefore one would participate in the power in that place that is less in one's own. A fascinating Christian writing from the fourth century is called the *Pilgrimage of Egeria*. This is about a Spanish nun, a Spanish woman religious, who with a band of other women go on a trip, believe it or not, to the "Holy Land," which is what they call it. They visit Mount Sinai, and there's a tour guide who shows them the sites. They visit Jerusalem to see the places where Jesus lies, and Egeria wants to go to Tarsus and Seleucia, not because she wants to see the tomb of Saint Paul, but because she wants to see the tomb of Saint Thecla, the patroness of women. We see sort of a very interesting proto-feminism within Christianity with Egeria. This theme of pilgrimage grows in popularity through the ages, and continues today with pilgrimage to Rome, pilgrimage to other holy places.

A further development of the sanctification of space is worship that would take place at the tombs of the martyrs. Again, since the martyrs were holy people, sanctified through their witness, then the place where they died, or the place where they were buried, must have more power. Christians would gather there, celebrate the Eucharist at those places, burn candles, and have pilgrimage to those sites.

A further extension of this, and you see how this grows, are relics. That is, if the place is holy, then if I touch the place with a physical object, or better yet, if I have a piece of bone of the martyr, or a piece of cloth that touched the martyr, or the spot, then I can carry that somewhat as a good luck charm, as something holy that I can put in a bracelet, put around my neck as a sort of an amulet. We see this continuous expansion.

Finally, there are holy icons, or holy pictures of saints, and of Jesus, which are thought to communicate the divine. Thus, the establishment of Christianity made a difference. It made a difference in terms of Christianity's place in the world, politically, but it also enabled Christianity to begin to create a distinctively Christian culture through the multiple ways of sanctifying both space and time.

Moral Teaching
Lecture 7

Christianity has struggled mightily to shape a consistent moral message that is consonant with its central religious experiences and convictions.

Compared to other Western religions, the moral teaching of Christianity is complex and, in some respects, confusing. Both Judaism and Islam are committed to law (Torah, Shariah) as the adequate expression of moral values. Christianity, in contrast, has struggled to shape a consistent moral message that is consonant with its central experiences and convictions. In part, this is the result of an ambivalence about the law, grounded in the experience of Jesus as one condemned by the norm of Torah. In part, this is due to Christianity's early experience of the Holy Spirit and personal transformation into the image of Christ. In part, this stems from Christianity's beginning as a persecuted sect rather than as a vision for society at large. In part, this arises from the severe conflicts of the 2nd century around issues of asceticism.

As it developed, Christianity drew on three main sources for its moral teaching. (1) The Law of Moses (Torah) continued to play a key role in shaping Christian morality. Christians distinguished (as Jews did not) between the ritual commandments, which no longer applied, and the moral commandments, which did. In particular, Christians accepted the binding force of the Ten Commandments (Exod. 20:2–27; Deut. 5:6–21) and the commandment to love the neighbor as the self (Lev. 19:18). (2) The teaching of Jesus in the Gospels, especially the Sermon on the Mount (Matt. 5–7) is regarded as of central importance for Christian morality. Jesus is understood as reinterpreting Torah through interiorization, intensification, and radicalization. Jesus identifies as the two "great commandments" the love of God and the love of neighbor (see Matt. 22:34–40). Jesus issues a call to discipleship that demands radical renunciation of parents, property, and marriage. And (3) The experience of the Holy Spirit consequent on the Resurrection of Jesus served as both the source and shaper of moral life (Galatians 5:25). Both virginity and martyrdom can be seen as bodily expressions of belief in the resurrection life. The Spirit enabled believers to have "the mind of Christ" (1 Cor. 2:16) that guided their moral reasoning. An emphasis on interior disposition made the following of one's conscience, rather than an external norm, paramount (1 Cor. 8–10).

From the start, Christianity has also drawn on other moral norms to supplement the three main authorities. In the New Testament itself, Greco-Roman moral exhortation finds expression in the lists of vices and virtues, in the tables of household ethics, and in the appropriation of such ideals as contentment or self-sufficiency. In the medieval period, Scholastic moral theology made extensive use of Aristotle's ethics of virtue. At times, Christian moral teaching has been closely linked to ecclesiastical law, leading to forms of moral casuistry.

The writings of the New Testament are ill-fitted to providing moral guidance for a society.

The struggle for a consistent public moral stance has characterized Christianity for much of its history. Christianity's first focus as a struggling sect was on its own identity vis-à-vis Judaism and Hellenism, rather than on legislating for society as a whole. The writings of the New Testament are ill-fitted to providing moral guidance for a society. Christians have adopted a spectrum of positions, from the absolute renunciation of the world to ruling the world. The fundamental struggle for most Christians today is between a highly individualistic ethic (spirituality) and a highly engaged ethic (liberation/ political theology). ■

Essential Reading

Gospel of Matthew, 5–7.

W. A. Meeks, *The Origins of Christian Morality: The First Two Centuries* (New Haven: Yale University Press, 1993).

Supplemental Reading

R. B. Hays, *The Moral Vision of the New Testament: Community, Cross, New Creation: A Contemporary Introduction to New Testament Ethics* (San Francisco: HarperSanFrancisco, 1996).

A. Verhey, *Remembering Jesus: Christian Community, Scripture, and the Moral Life* (Grand Rapids: Eerdmans, 2002).

Questions to Consider

1. Why has Christianity struggled to construct a coherent moral teaching?

2. How adequately does "the law of love" comprehend Christian ethics?

Moral Teaching
Lecture 7—Transcript

In the definition of religious experience from Joachim Wach that I used in my first presentation, I distinguished religious experience from ascetic experience in terms of the final criterion that religious experience issues an appropriate action.

In the last presentation, we saw one way in which Christians translated the religious experience of Jesus into appropriate action, namely through the organization of space and time through worship. This means not only the worship of the Eucharist, which is one of the seven sacraments, but also the other six sacraments of baptism, confirmation, marriage, holy orders, reconciliation, and final anointing.

In this session, I look at another way in which Christians have seen the experience of Jesus Christ issue in appropriate action, namely the way in which they have tried to structure their lives ethically.

We turn to Christian practice number two, moral teaching. Compared to other Western religious traditions, the moral teaching of Christianity is both complex, which we've grown to expect, but is also in many ways confusing. Both Judaism and Islam are committed to law. In Judaism, it is the Torah, and in Islam, the Shariah, as perfectly adequate expressions of moral values. Through Moses, God revealed Torah to the Jewish people, and that law has been the basis for the interpretation of Jewish practice and morality throughout the ages.

Similarly, the revelation of Allah to Muhammad through the Qur'an is combined by Islamic scholars with the Hadith—the stories of the prophet's practice—into a system of law, Shariah, which is regarded as an adequate expression of Islamic morality. Thus, for Muslims to be *Islama*, that is, to be truly submissive to Allah, they must observe the law. For Jews to be faithful to God means observing Torah.

Christianity, in contrast, has struggled mightily to shape a consistent moral message that is consonant with its central religious experiences and convictions. There are probably more, but I will give you four reasons for this difficulty.

The first reason is the ambivalence that Christians had from the beginning with law. First, Jesus, according to the Gospels, was not an observer of the Jewish law. He broke the Sabbath. He associated with those people who did break the commandments, the sinners and tax collectors, and his death was one that Torah itself condemned as one cursed by God. Deuteronomy 21:23 says, "Cursed be everyone who hangs upon a tree."

This ambivalence about the law is further thematized in several of Paul's letters, especially Galatians and Romans. In response to early Jewish Christians who think that circumcision is required and are convincing Gentile Christians that circumcision and the observance of the law is a higher status within Christianity, Paul declares that it is faith and not the works of the law that ought to be the norm for Christian life. Therefore, there is ambivalence about how law can work for Christians.

Indeed, Christians, especially in the Protestant tradition, who based their sense of Christianity primarily on the letters of Paul, frequently have a great deal of trouble in thinking about law as an appropriate way of expressing morality. There is a kind of an empty nomian theme that runs through much of Christianity.

The second reason is that part of the early Christian experience was the experience of a Holy Spirit, as we have seen, this experience of empowerment and of personal transformation in the image of Christ. If Christ was a lawbreaker, if Christ's death was cursed by the law, what does it mean to be transformed into the image of Jesus Christ? The law is heteronomous. It is a norm outside of us. The Holy Spirit is autonomous. It is a norm inside the person.

The third problem is that Christianity began its existence, as we saw, as a persecuted sect, as a persecuted minority whose first concern was primarily with tending the community, and not developing a vision for society as a whole. In this struggle, it faced certain intrinsic problems.

For example, Jesus was not a lawgiver. Jesus's own teachings were parabolic. They were critical. They were delivered often in the form of snappy aphorisms, but they did not provide a vision of how people should structure their lives.

When Christianity moved into the larger Greco-Roman world, it found itself in something of a parasitic relationship to Jewish and Greco-Roman culture, and had to develop its morality in conversation with those two larger traditions.

The fourth reason why Christians have struggled to develop a consistent morality, are the severe conflicts of the second century in the debate with Gnosticism. We saw that Christianity explicitly rejected the cosmic dualism and the severe asceticism that was demanded by teachers like Marcion and Valentinus.

Explicitly, Christians affirm the value of the body, the value of sexuality, the value of marriage and of having children, but implicitly it has struggled with what might be called the virus of Gnosticism that nevertheless continues to percolate within the Christian system. Christians have notoriously had difficulty with such things as the body, with pleasure, and above all—with sexuality.

These are some of the factors that have made it very difficult for Christians to have a clear and consistent moral teaching, just as the fundamental experience of Christianity as the new life that is offered through the Resurrection of an executed criminal is paradoxical. Therefore, it is not at all clear how that experience should lead to an appropriate moral behavior.

As Christianity developed, it drew on three main sources for its moral teaching. In the first place, the Law of Moses, or Torah, continued to play a key role in shaping Christian morality despite the ambivalence that I mentioned earlier. Indeed, I think it is difficult to overemphasize the fundamental and continuing importance of the structure of Torah for Christian moral thinking. What do I mean by the structure of Torah?

What I mean is that human beings see themselves first of all in a relationship with God. That is called a "covenant." This is a binding relationship of loyalty, so that morality is thought of not in terms of simply becoming a certain kind of person, as in Greco-Roman ethics, but rather as a response to the divine being, as a personal response of obedience or disobedience.

Secondly, this covenant is articulated in terms of observances which express God's will, the commandments and so forth, and by doing these things, one pleases God by showing obedience and loyalty, just as one pleases a father. If God is father, God reveals what God wants humans to do, and humans please God by that kind of response. Christian ethics, like Jewish ethics, is fundamentally theological ethics. Thus, Christian sense of morality is not defined specifically in terms of virtue and vice, but in terms of sin and faith, because faith is the fundamental response to the deity—positive response—and sin is disobedience. It is that rupture of that relationship through immoral behavior. The framework of Torah remains enduringly important for Christianity.

When Christians looked at the Law of Moses—which as you remember is very extensive and includes all kinds of prescriptions—for worship, for diet, and so forth for purity regulations, what the early Christians did was make a distinction that Jews do not. For Jews, all of the *mitzvos* are equally important. Observing dietary regulations is just as important in terms of pleasing God as not committing adultery is.

Christians distinguished between what they regarded as moral commandments—above all the Ten Commandments, which had an enduring normative force—and what they called ritual commandments—circumcision, purity, diet, and worship—which they regarded as having been abrogated by the experience of Jesus. Christians still regard the Ten Commandments as normative for their lives, but do not take seriously the ritual commandments of Torah. These tend to be interpreted by Christians symbolically or allegorically. Thus, circumcision is not the physical snipping of the foreskin, but the purity of heart or a good intention by which one responds to God.

In particular, the Christians accept the binding force of the Ten Commandments, but they do so in combination, interestingly, with Leviticus 19:18, which is the commandment to love the neighbor as the self. This combination of the Ten Commandments and love of neighbor is, from the first, regarded as essential for Christians.

In his letter to the Romans, in chapter 13, verse 8, following, Paul says to the Roman congregation, "Owe no one anything except to love one another. For the one who loves another has fulfilled the law. The commandments: you shall not commit adultery, you shall not murder, you shall not steal, you shall not covet," he's clearly alluding to the Ten Commandments, "and any other commandment are summed up in this one word"—are recapitulated in this one word—"love your neighbor as yourself," Leviticus 19:18. "Love does no wrong to a neighbor, therefore love is the fulfilling of the law," and this has been a very important principle, that the supreme law for Christians is the law of love.

The great value, however, of negative commandments: "Do not do this, do not do that, and do not do that," is that they are definite. When you are told, "Do not commit murder," you are forbidden to do one thing, but you are allowed to give life in all kinds of ways and to affirm life in all kinds of ways.

The difficulty with positive commandments, such as "Keep holy the Sabbath," is, "When do I quit? When have I done enough to keep the Sabbath holy?" They tend to become very complicated and ambiguous. It's the same thing with the law of love.

Christians have struggled with: "What is the meaning of love? It's not a feeling. It's not simply an attitude. Somehow, it has to be translated into action, but who is my neighbor? What does it mean to love my neighbor? What are the limits of what I need to give to my neighbor?" These are complicated issues for Christians.

The second main source for moral teaching in Christianity is the teaching of Jesus. In the Gospels, especially The Sermon on the Mount, as it is called in the Gospel of Matthew, chapter 5 through 7, and there is another version of this in the Gospel of Luke, chapter 6. Many Christians regard The Sermon on the Mount to be of central importance for Christian morality. Jesus there is understood as reinterpreting Torah in terms of his own messianic message, and he does this in three ways. The pattern is consistent throughout. "You have heard it said," and then Jesus quotes something from Torah, and then he responds, "But I say to you."

The various antitheses show us three ways of Jesus dealing with the law. One is interiorizing it. "You have heard it said, do not commit adultery, but I say to you, do not lust even in the heart against a woman." "You have heard it said, do not murder, but I say to you, do not be angry;" this is probably better translated as "do not be hostile toward the other." Anger is an emotion; hostility is an attitude.

There is also a kind of intensification. "You have heard it said that you can give your wife in divorce; I say to you, 'No divorce.'" "You have heard it said that you can take an oath upon these grounds or those grounds, but I say take no oaths at all." That's actually making the law more stringent.

Finally, he radicalizes Torah. "If a neighbor takes something from you, do not take revenge. Rather, give him even more." "Do not love just the person who loves you, but love your enemy." This is a more radical extension of the commandment of Leviticus 19:15, which basically applied to fellow Israelites. These sayings in the Sermon on the Mount have been one of the bases of Christian morality.

Again in the Gospels, we see that in the mouth of Jesus, the basic command of loving God and loving neighbor are united in Matthew, chapter 22, verses 34-40. We find Jesus responding to some Pharisees who ask him, "What is the greatest commandment in the Law?" This is sort of a trick question. By responding, "You shall love the Lord your God with all your heart, and all your soul, and all your mind. This is the greatest and first commandment." This is the *Shma Yisrael* that we talked about two presentations ago. "A second is like it: 'You shall love your neighbor as yourself.'" "On these two commandments," Matthew has Jesus say, "hang the law and the prophets." In other words, this summarizes everything. These are devotion to God, and love for one's fellow human person.

The problem with Jesus's sayings as a norm for morality for Christians is that he says a lot of other things as well. Many of them are quite disturbing, so Jesus issues demands of discipleship that require a radical renunciation of parents, of property, and of marriage. I'll take up this radical edge of Jesus's teaching in our next presentation. For now, we simply add to Torah the sayings of Jesus as a norm for Christian morality.

The third norm to which Christians have appealed for their moral teaching is the experience of the Holy Spirit that is consequent on the Resurrection of Jesus from the dead. The spirit was thought to be not only a source of life, but also, if you will, an illumination or an enhancement of consciousness that enabled one to live in a certain fashion. Paul says in Galatians, "If you live by the spirit, then also walk by the spirit." He uses the term there that could actually be translated in Jewish terms as let the spirit be your norm for your life.

In this regard, both virginity and martyrdom, which are very important ways of using the body in early Christianity, can be seen as specific ways in which the Holy Spirit leads people to witness to the Resurrection. If one says, "I will remain a virgin, or celibate. I will not engage in active sexual life. I will not have children, but out of my commitment to God, I will remain celibate," one is testifying to the power of God to give life beyond biological regeneration clearly.

The same thing is true of martyrdom. If I am willing to give my life in witness to a truth, this is connected in early Christianity to a belief in the Resurrection—that God is able to bring others from the dead as he raised Jesus from the dead. Thus, even Jesus's death is seen as this kind of martyrdom or witness.

Even in more ordinary life, however, in the lives that Christians live together, the Holy Spirit was regarded as a sort of guide that enabled Christians to understand how to make decisions. Paul tells the Corinthians that they have not received the spirit of this world, but they have received the spirit of God to enable them to understand the things that God has given them. He concludes that passage in I Corinthians, chapter 2, verse 16, by saying, "We have the mind of Christ." In other words, there is a certain mindset, or way of thinking, that is that of Jesus himself, that Christians are able to interiorize or internalize, and live in that fashion.

The pattern, then, of behavior is one that is an imitation of Jesus. Paul says, "If you live by the spirit, bear one another's burdens, and thus fulfill the law of Christ." He says this in Galatians, chapter 6, verse 2. This pattern of the Messiah: What is that pattern? It's the pattern of radical love. Jesus was radically obedient to God and gave his life in service to others as a gift to others. "This is my body given for you. This is my blood poured out for you." To think like Jesus, if you will, is to be somebody who thinks in terms not solipsistically or selfishly, not in terms of one's own projects, but in terms of the larger good of the community, a form of altruism.

This emphasis on internal disposition, and on internal transformation, made the following of one's own conscience extremely important, rather than external norms. Here I would refer you to Paul's exquisite discussion in I Corinthians, chapters 8 through 10, as he walks through the problem of whether or not one should eat foods that have been offered to idols.

On one side of the question he insists that each person's individual conscience is the determinant of the morality of his or her action. This is an extraordinarily important principle that becomes the basis of jurisprudence in the West, that what I think an action is constitutes the morality of the action. If I kill somebody, but I do not know that I'm killing somebody, or I do not intend to kill that person, then that's not murder in the same way that an intention to kill is. That's interior conscience.

Then Paul complicates that, however, by saying that even though you have the right to follow your conscience, if this should hurt your neighbor, you give up that right. There is this altruism, looking to the needs of the other even if the other is stupid.

Finally, he extends his argument to say that while it is true that you have the absolute right to do this, if a neighbor is not present, you should be careful. Even though idols are not real, idolatry is, and your behavior can involve you in systems of evil that go beyond individual actions. Paul's moral thinking here is complex, intricate, and sophisticated.

The Law of Moses, the teachings of Jesus, and the direction of the Holy Spirit have been norms for morality for Christians, but they don't always agree on every point, and it's not quite clear how they fit together. Because of this, from the start, Christianity has also had to draw upon other moral norms to supplement these three main authorities.

In the New Testament itself, we see the use of Greco-Roman moral exhortation. For example, when Paul talks about those who are being baptized in I Corinthians, chapter 6, verses 9-11, he refers to "the way you used to be," and he basically gives there a standard vice list that we would find among Greco-Roman philosophers, all these nasty ways of behaving, sexual to be sure, but also anti-social kinds of behaviors. In contrast, he then gives lists of virtues, the fruits of the spirit. How does the spirit act? These are positive ways of acting.

Paul also employs Greco-Roman moral teaching in describing the household ethics. How should husbands and wives interact with each other? How should parents be with children? How should slaves be with masters? From the beginning, we see the use of Greco-Roman moral teaching in order to supplement the spirit, the teachings of Jesus, and Torah. Indeed, early Christian moral teaching resembles in many ways stoic ethics in terms of its rigor, and in terms of its concern for doing the right thing.

In the medieval church, Scholastic moral theology made even more extensive use of Aristotle, and Aristotle's moral theology, which is a character ethic. Its focus is not on, "What do I do?" That's pretty clear. By that time, Christianity had pretty well laid out—in great detail—what were the things to be done.

The issue was, "What kind of person can I be? What is my character? What is my intention?" To fill out that side of ethics, Scholastic theology made great use of Aristotle's ethics as found in the *Nicomachean Ethics*, in particular.

Also in the Middle Ages, Christian moral teaching has been closely linked to ecclesiastical law, which leads to forms of moral casuistry. We will see that this is one of the problems that the Protestant Reformation had with Catholicism. We saw in our last presentation how elaborate the hierarchy and the sacramental system of Christianity became. Accompanying that, quite naturally as a matter of course, is the development of law, specifically canon law or church law, as directives. How do we carry out worship? How do we fast? How do we observe holy days?

What happens in this form of moral casuistry and making these little decisions is that church regulations and genuine moral obligations tend to merge one into the other in a fairly confusing fashion. Thus, we get to the anomaly of Roman Catholics, when I was growing up, of thinking that if they didn't fast on Friday, they had fundamentally committed a mortal transgression, and displeased God. They would have to confess that as a sin. That's purely a church regulation that had taken on a moral valence. There's a lot of confusion that entered into the complexity of Christian moral teaching as it developed.

In particular, let me turn at the end of this presentation to one of the fundamental struggles within Christianity, which is that of a consistent public moral stance. As we saw, Christianity's first experience as a struggling sect was its own identity vis-à-vis Judaism and Hellenism. "How can we be a holy people? How can we be the saints over and against the world?" It was a counter-cultural phenomenon. It wasn't legislating for society. It was ill prepared to become the legislator for the imperial system.

The writings of the New Testament are so diverse, and are so historically conditioned that they are ill-fitted to provide moral guidance for an entire society. Christians have, over and over again, experienced precisely this kind of difficulty. First of all, the New Testament doesn't address a great many things that a society needs to have addressed. It doesn't describe what

Christian music should be like, or what Christian educational systems should be like. How should bridges be built? It simply is not a law book in that sense in the way, in fact, that the Qur'an is, or even that the Law of Moses is, showing how agriculture should be carried out. It doesn't talk about a lot of things that need to be talked about.

Secondly, what it does talk about, it tends to talk about in a counter-cultural way, rather than in a way that builds society. Can you really not have any kind of divorce, and still survive? Even in the New Testament, we find Christians struggling with the severity of Jesus's commandment on divorce. Maybe there are some exceptions.

Because these are written for a Greco-Roman society, they also say things that are very difficult for Christians to live by. For example, they certainly approve of slavery, and Christians have had to struggle with that in terms of the wider spectrum of society. If you look at the New Testament, and you say, "What does the New Testament have to say about X?" the right answer is usually, "What did you read last?" It has very different views on how one should regard, for example, the governance of the state. In Romans 13, and in I Peter, the emperor is fine. "Obey the emperor. The emperor is a good person." If you read the Book of Revelation, chapter 17, the emperor and Rome, the imperial power is a great beast that enslaves people, and you should resist it with all of your might.

It is very difficult to construct a coherent Christian social ethic, and so Christians today tend to find themselves struggling between two extremes morally. On the one side, Christians tend to opt for a highly individualistic morality, a sort of a cultivation of the self. They take care in their sexual behavior, their familial relations, and their emotions. This is, of course, especially true in First-World countries, where we're comfortable enough to be able to nurture the self as a moral agent, and in many cases that sort of individualistic ethic is perfectly comfortable with baptizing capitalism and forces of aggression, and of competition, and so forth.

On the other side, you have those who opt for a highly engaged ethic, liberation theology in particular, which sees sin not in terms of people's individual morality, but in oppressive and evil social structures. They do everything they can in order to combat the oppression of the poor, sexism and the oppression of women, the oppression of children, and the enslavement of people economically. Their sense of moral mission is to change the social structures of society in the name of Christ.

The Radical Edge
Lecture 8

Throughout its history, certain Christians looked to elements in the New Testament that pointed to a more radical form of discipleship as warrant for their pursuit of a more heroic path.

The battle for self-definition in the 2nd century made "the great church" a public organization that included people with a wide range of commitment and fervor. The orthodox party rejected the position of the Gnostics that only the "enlightened" (or *pneumatic*) were saved, while the *psychic* had some chance, and the "ordinary people" (the *hylic*) had no future. The subsequent establishment of the church under Constantine, the safe and even privileged place of the church, encouraged membership with minimal commitment.

Certain Christians have appealed to elements in the New Testament that pointed to a more radical form of discipleship as a warrant for their pursuit of a more heroic path.l. The letters of Paul contain certain utopian tendencies, such as the breakdown of ethnic, gender, and class differences, that stand in tension with life in the Hellenistic household. The story of Jesus presents an itinerant preacher, and some of his sayings demand the rejection of family and possessions and the willingness to "bear the cross" after him. The Book of Acts portrays the ideal church in terms of a complete sharing of possessions.

The Book of Revelation envisages a community of saints and prophets who resist the political and economic power of the great beast. Jesus appears to be asexual and dies violently as a martyr; Paul is not married and dies violently as a martyr; Peter dies as a martyr; and virginity, martyrdom, and poverty are holy qualities for early Christians.

Many of those called "saints" in the Christian tradition have, in various ways, sought to challenge not only the way of the world but also too comfortable an existence within the church. In the first centuries, martyrdom and virginity were modes of testifying to a radical belief in the Resurrection and a resistance to conventional notions of success or salvation. From at least the 3rd century forward, many have espoused the ideal of *fuga mundi* ("flee the world") in a variety of monastic forms. Hermits and anchorites live in complete or semi-solitude, devoting their lives to prayer. The sayings of the hermits (aphoristic words of wisdom) are currently enjoying popularity among those seeking to expand their spiritual lives. A major development in monasticism was the work of Benedict of Nursia, who wrote a rule for monks to live in celibate communities organized around shared possessions, work, and prayer.

> **Missionaries have carried the gospel to foreign lands in obedience to the command of Jesus to "make disciples of all nations." (Matt. 28:20)**

Mendicants and millenarians have likewise embodied a radical vision of Christian existence. Mendicants imitated the poverty of Jesus and depended on the support of others who are less radical in lifestyle. The first mendicant was Saint Francis of Assisi, who founded the Franciscan order. Millenarian Christians have taken the Book of Revelation very seriously and have organized their lives in anticipation of that book's vision of the imminent coming of Jesus by instituting a community of possessions on earth. (See Thomas Muentzer and the radical Reformation in Germany.) This belief often leads to disaster, as exemplified in recent history by the tragedy of David Koresh and the Branch Davidians.

Paul becomes a great missionary to the Gentiles, going on three missionary journeys throughout Syria, Asia Minor, Macedonia, and Achaia.

Missionaries have carried the gospel to foreign lands in obedience to the command of Jesus to "make disciples of all nations" (Matt. 28:20), experiencing as a result, the same persecution, separation from family, and poverty.

Another manifestation of the "radical edge" in Christianity, though subtler, is the practice of mysticism. In every religion, mysticism represents the effort to seek an unmediated access to the divine presence and power. By its nature, mysticism threatens the ordinary structures of sacred mediation. Jesus and Paul were themselves undoubtedly mystics, and the history of Christianity is punctuated by a variety of forms of mysticism. Radical forms of Christianity have served as catalysts of reform, but they have also, at times, served as causes of division. ■

Essential Reading

Benedict of Nursia, *Rule for Monks*.

Supplemental Reading

J. Aumann et. al., *Monasticism: A Historical Overview* (Still River, MA: St. Bede's Publications, 1984).

W. H. C. Frend, *Martyrdom and Persecution in the Early Church* (Garden City: Anchor Books, 1967).

B. McGinn, *The Presence of God: A History of Western Christian Mysticism*, 3 vols. (New York: Crossroad, 2000).

Questions to Consider

1. What elements of continuity can be discerned among martyrdom, monasticism, and mysticism?

2. How does the "radical edge" in Christianity serve both as a catalyst to reform and as a threat to stability?

The Radical Edge
Lecture 8—Transcript

One of the ways in which religion is interesting is the way in which it tends to stabilize the world. By its very nature, religion, which gives an account of how things are, tends to be conservative and helps preserve the way things are.

Like other religions, Christianity has a great deal within it that stabilizes the world and supports the order of things. The Christian story, we have seen, creates a coherent understanding of the world, and of the human place within it, and of the destiny of the world and of human destiny. The Christian creed articulates that vision in terms of a God who is intrinsically involved with humans and promises them a share in God's life. The Christian church and the sacraments provide a secure sense of sacred time and sacred space. However complex, we saw in the last lecture that Christian moral teaching also provides guidance for Christians in their behavior.

Religion also has another aspect that is more disruptive, however. Christianity also has that dimension which is more destabilizing of the world, and more destabilizing of the tradition. Today, we talk about the Christian practice, the "radical edge."

That great battle for self-definition with Gnosticism, I always go back to Gnosticism; the great battle with Gnosticism in the second century made the great church a public organization, and also included people with a wide range of commitment and fervor. You will remember that Gnosticism and part of Gnosticism's appeal to many was that it divided humanity into three groups, one of which was the group of the elite, or the "enlightened," the Gnostics themselves, who would, because they had the spark of awareness, flee back to the light and just let their bodies be shed.

Then in the middle ground were the *psychics*, people with some possibility of getting to the point of being enlightened.

The vast majority of humans, however, were the *hylic*, the mud people, with no possibility for enlightenment, simply the herd, if you will.

In rejecting that sort of elitist vision of Christianity, the Orthodox Church opened itself to all levels of humanity: Not only the smart, but the ignorant; not only the powerful, but the powerless; and so forth. Christianity thought of itself as being catholic with a small "c," that is, having a universal embrace. What happened as a result, however, is that what it gained in universality, it lost in terms of edge, or in terms of excellence.

When Christianity was subsequently made the established church of the Roman Empire, the imperial religion under Constantine, the safe and even privileged position of the church encouraged membership with minimal commitment. The age of martyrs was over; the church was even an advantageous organization to belong to. To have been a bishop was to have held a public, and even significant, social status within the Empire.

This kind of safety, on one side, was good news. We were glad we weren't all being killed. The persecution was difficult, and martyrdom appeals mainly to those who have difficulties.

With safety, however, also arises the danger of smugness and of mediocrity. What happens to Christianity's edge? What happens to those who want to be excellent within Christianity? Is to be Christian simply to be somebody who has a place in the world, and that's it?

Throughout its history since the time of Constantine, certain Christians have appealed to elements in the New Testament that pointed to a more radical form of discipleship as a warrant for their pursuit of a more heroic path, a more impressive way of being Christian, if you will.

The letters of Paul contain, as we have seen, many elements that are stabilizing and affirming of the basic Greco-Roman household, and the Greco-Roman Empire. Paul in Romans 13 and in Titus, chapter 2, holds out the vision of good citizenship within the Empire. He develops the tables of household ethics, which are fundamentally conservative with respect to the hierarchical status of male over female, parents over children, and masters over slaves. He affirms marriage as a powerful agent of good, indeed, as a symbol of Christ and the church. All of these tend in the conservative direction.

There are also elements in Paul of a more utopian vision, of a more radical understanding of the Christian community, however. This is found above all in Galatians 3:28, where Paul says that, "In Christ, there is neither male nor female, neither Jew nor Greek, neither slave nor free." He breaks down the three great status markers of antiquity: The difference between male and female; ethnicity, Jew/Greek; and social status, slave or free. He said none of that matters. This is a little bit, this egalitarian vision, is a little bit more radical than living within the household as a member of a family. How do you put those two things together?

Likewise, Paul holds out the vision that people are empowered within the community because of the gift of the Holy Spirit, not because of their age, and not because of their office. Again, this is a more disruptive element. If we took seriously the fact that even the youngest or the least educated among us might be powerfully gifted by the Holy Spirit with wisdom, rather than the official priest or minister, that's a disruptive element, and a destabilizing element within the community. Paul offers some hints of a more radical version of Christianity.

The story of Jesus, obviously, also presents such hints. Jesus, after all, is an itinerant preacher. He is not a teacher who is within a home. He's on the road. He's on the road with a group of followers who depend upon the gifts of others, in order to support themselves. Some of Jesus's sayings seem to demand a commitment in order to be a follower of his, that means the rejection of family and possessions, and the willingness to be the kind of person he was, that is, to "bear the cross" after him.

He says of himself, "The Son of Man does not have a place to lay his head." He calls his disciples to follow him. He says that "whoever wishes to come after me must give up father and mother, hate father and mother, and give up all their possessions and follow me." He tells a rich young man who approaches him and asks him, "What should I do for eternal life?" and

Jesus answers by saying, "Keep the commandments." The man says, "I've done all that. What else can I do?" Jesus responds by saying, "If you want to be perfect, come follow me, selling all your possessions." A life of radical poverty seems to be demanded by Jesus.

Likewise, in the Gospel of Matthew 19:11 and 12, immediately after Jesus talks about no divorce at all, his disciples respond by saying, "Well, this is hard. It would be better for a person not to get married at all, if they can't be divorced." Jesus responds by talking about being a eunuch for the Kingdom of Heaven. That is, being a person who is asexual in order to fulfill the demands of being a disciple of Jesus. Again, the sayings of Jesus hold out certain radical demands that seem to be impossible of fulfillment if one is part of a family, one is part of a household, or a citizen of a state. Thirdly, the Book of Acts, in its description of the earliest Christians—immediately after Pentecost, when everybody was filled with the Holy Spirit—says that all of the believers were of one spirit, and were united in mind and heart, and they shared all their possessions. No one who had anything called it his own, but they held all things in common.

In describing the earliest community as a community of possessions, Luke is echoing the utopian ideal of Greek philosophy, as found already in Plato, that the perfect city state is one in which everybody is friends, and everybody has possessions in common; therefore, nobody really owns any private property. If we took that description of the church in Acts as normative, we would say Christians must be communists. Christians must be socialists; that is, there is no private property, but everybody holds everything in common. That's a pretty radical vision as well.

The Book of Revelation portrays the Roman state, as I said in the last lecture, as the great beast, the whore of Babylon, which takes prisoners through its economic and political power, enslaves people, and oppresses them. The Christian community—which is thought of in terms of being servants and saints and prophets—is commanded, "Worship God only." In other words, Jesus is the King of Kings and the Lord of Lords. If the community worships God alone, they will resist the sovereignty of the imperial power. This is quite different than Paul saying, "Be a good citizen. Obey the emperor." This is saying, "Resist the emperor. Form a counter community of worship that resists the societal power of economics and of politics."

Those are four kinds of radical themes that run through the New Testament, and let me add a fifth. Finally, we have the striking fact that Jesus himself is a remarkably asexual creature. There is no indication that he has any sexual relations with anybody, so he's a virgin, and he dies violently as a martyr. Paul, his most powerful Apostle, is not married. Paul says, "I wish everybody could be like I am, but everybody has his own gift from God. One person this, the other person that." Paul is unmarried. Paul dies violently as a martyr. Peter had a wife, but he also dies as a martyr.

Thus, we have this image of the earliest leaders of the church, that is who took it most seriously, not as people who lived in households, not people who married, not people who kept their jobs, that donated a bit to the community chest, but rather the real heroes of the faith. The people who are most like Jesus were people who hit the road; people who gave up their possessions; people who gave up any ordinary human relationships, left their families, and didn't form a new family.

For Christians who were bored or horrified by the smugness and safety that came upon the church from the time of Constantine, there were these passages and these examples that they could appeal to, to push them to a more heroic form of Christian life. Thus, many of those called saints within the Christian tradition have in various ways sought to challenge not simply the way of society at large, but even the rest of the church, to challenge the church itself as being too comfortable a way of living.

In the first three centuries, which we have called alternatively, the "Age of Persecution," and the "Age of Martyrdom," the two things obviously go together; virginity and martyrdom were frequently found among these church leaders. Ignatius of Antioch was martyred. Polycarp was martyred. Even though the church, as a whole, was regarded as a community of the saints, preeminently, the holy ones were those who finished the task, if you will, by committing their lives wholly to God through poverty, chastity, and the form of obedience and loyalty that would issue in death.

Ignatius tells the Roman community when he is being hauled there in chains to face his martyrdom, "Don't interfere. Don't try to save me, because I will not be a complete Christian until I have shared in the suffering and death of Christ." There is a kind of martyr piety. When, in the martyrdom of Polycarp, the description of martyrdom of Polycarp's martyrdom is one in which he has a vision as he dies, of participation in the Eucharist, in the body and blood of Christ. He is like bread being baked in an oven, an illusion to being fully incorporated into the reality of Christ.

This is not just in that earliest period. If we take Christianity's earliest and greatest theologian, Origen of Alexandria, whose dates are 184 to 254, late in the second and well into the third century, Origen's father was martyred when Origen was just a boy. Origen, himself, longed for martyrdom. Indeed, he wrote a tractate on martyrdom to encourage people not to resist, and to be willing to die as a martyr. He, himself, was not killed for the faith, but he was technically a confessor. He was tortured to the point where his health was utterly broken, and he died shortly thereafter. Origen lived a life of virginity. More than that, according to Eusebius of Caesarea, Origen took so seriously Jesus's line about becoming a eunuch for the Kingdom of Heaven that he castrated himself, in order to become asexual. He lived a life of poverty, and he wrote voluminously. Ancient authorities disagree as to whether or not he wrote 6,000 treatises, or 2,000 treatises, or only 800 treatises. In any case, you can see the good effects of that kind of concentration. If all of your energies are poured into that, you can be an extremely prolific author.

From the time of Constantine forward, many Christians imitated the example of Greco-Roman philosophical schools, and that Jewish example of a philosophical school called the Essene Community at Qumran, and went into the wilderness in order to pursue a more rigorous form of Christian existence. Their slogan was, in Latin, *fuga mundi*, "flee from the world." Notice, the world is urban. The world is civilization. It is a place of corruption, sophistication, comfort, and all of these things.

So, St. Anthony, in the early fourth century, read the passage in the Gospel about giving up all one's possessions, and he did that. He left his family, sold all his possessions, and went out and lived as a hermit in the desert. He was followed. This is, of course, one of the paradoxes; hermits tend to become popular. He was followed out into the desert by others who lived alone out there. These were our earliest forms of monasticism in the church, with the word "monk" coming from the word *monos* in Greek, meaning "alone." The original image of being a monk was of a life of solitude devoted completely to, obviously, a subsistence existence out in the wilderness, to silence—some monks would not speak for years—and to prayer—silent meditation, prayer, the recitation of the Psalms.

Some of the fathers of the desert recited the entire Psalter every day, all 150 Psalms, as a form of prayer. Slowly, in the desert of Scetis in Egypt, there developed a form of life that was called "semi-heremetical," in other words, part hermit, part social.

In the desert of Scetis, each monk would have his own cave, or own cell, and stay in silence and in solitude, but they would come together for communal prayer and communal meals, in silence, and then leave and go back to their own places again. This was a very popular form of monasticism for both males and females.

We have the wonderful *Conferences* of John Cassian written in the beginning of the fourth century, which are sermons delivered by various *abba*, various fathers of the desert. There were also mothers of the desert: women, widows, who would, with the deaths of their husbands (wealthy widows), sell their possessions and go out into the desert as is described in the *Lausiac History* by Palladius.

We also find that silence has a way of sharpening the tongue. We have a marvelous collection of the sayings of these desert fathers called the *Apophthegmata Patrum,* or "The Sayings of the Fathers," which have recently become very popular among Christians who are seeking the spiritual life. These are sharp one-liners, aphorisms, which contain a kind of gnomic wisdom that has been pondered in silence by these people who have devoted themselves completely to God.

A major development in Christian monasticism happened in the sixth century with Benedict of Nursia. Benedict of Nursia wrote a Rule for Monks. His vision for monasticism was not one of living alone, but rather one of living together, in what he called the "cenobitic" way of life. That word comes from the Greek, *koino-bios*, "the common life."

Benedict envisioned a kind of monasticism that wasn't quite so heroic, but was available to more ordinary people. Yes, there was silence, but there were times of speech. Yes, there were hardships, but basically, you dressed well, and you were fed three meals a day. You even got to drink a glass of wine a day. Yes, there was prayer, but only about seven hours of prayer a day. That was combined with good, healthy manual labor. "Prayer and work" was Benedict's motto. For Benedict, the hardest thing to do for people was to live together. He said that in his school of the Lord's service, he didn't want people to be spiritual athletes who could go the longest without eating or drinking or dress most shabbily. Rather, the difficulty of life together in an intentional community was Benedict's form of monasticism.

Benedictine monks and all of their offshoots were the re-civilizers of Europe. They were the ones who re-taught Europe how to read, how to farm, and so forth, in that long period that is sometimes called the Dark Ages. They also were the preservers of civilization through learning. Therefore, monasticism is a very important part of the history of Western civilization. This communal image of life is even found among Protestant groups, especially those of the Anabaptist tradition, for example, those called Hutterites, who are not celibate, but who live in communities, male and female, that share their possessions and share rural, agricultural work together.

Another form of the heroic way of life is found in mendicants and millenarians, who embody a radical vision of Christian existence. The mendicants appeared in the Middle Ages. The word "mendicant" means "a beggar." The first mendicant was St. Francis of Assisi at the end of the 12th and the beginning of the 13th century. He, and this is a classic story much like St. Anthony, read the words of Jesus: "Sell your possessions." He went out into the desert. St. Francis was the scion of a wealthy family of Assisi in Italy, very comfortable, and very carefree. The vision of the poor converted him. He tore off his wealthy clothes, he sold all of his possessions, and he committed himself to the life of a beggar, of wandering. His followers, called the Franciscans, devoted themselves to a life of radical poverty and dependence on others.

For Francis of Assisi, the image of poverty and of what he called the "Bambino," the poor baby Jesus, who was born in a stable, made him identify with the poor as a way of expressing the love of God. Francis of Assisi is one of the great heroes within the Christian tradition. He was so identified with Christ that he was a mystic. In fact, he is the first person we know about who had the *stigmata*: those marks of the cross, a psychosomatic expression of mystical experience—the bloody hands and feet and side that he developed when he was in middle age.

Millenarian Christians are those who take the vision of the Book of Revelation very seriously, and expect the near coming of Jesus. They, therefore, have tended to organize their lives as an anticipation of that coming of Jesus, soon.

We find this, for example, in the Radical Reformation in Munsler, Germany. People are expecting the new Jerusalem to occur, and they sell all their possessions, they live in common, and they wait in witness for the coming of the Lord. As I mentioned earlier, in an earlier presentation, Millennial Christianity is very much on the upsurge today. We find its expressions in a variety of forms, and very often, of course, it leads to disastrous experiences, as with David Koresh and the Branch Davidians in Waco a few years ago.

Another form of radical life that is too seldom appreciated is that of the missionaries. Again, as Jesus was an itinerant preacher, and Paul was an itinerant preacher, and as Jesus sent out people two-by-two carrying only a wallet and a staff, and one pair of sandals, and to rely upon what people would give them in order to proclaim the Kingdom of God, many Christians have taken seriously the commandment of Jesus to go make disciples of all nations. They have, in fact, gone to the very borders of civilization, whether it's St. Patrick in Ireland, St. Boniface in the Germanic Lands, or St. Cyril in Methodius in Slavic countries.

Christianity moved into new territories because of the willingness of these people to endure incredible hardships and dangers. Many of the martyrs were missionaries. As you know in the news, very recently, several missionaries in Yemen were killed who were trying to both proclaim the Kingdom of God, and to run a hospital and offer medical care. This was the experience of many missionaries, especially the French Catholic missionaries in North America, and the Spanish Catholic missionaries in Latin America.

This willingness to leave your family, or possibly take your family with you, go to a foreign land that's uncivilized, go into extraordinarily arduous circumstances in order to bring the message to others, is once more a radical witness to the call of Christ.

Finally, I want to talk about another manifestation of the "radical edge" in Christianity, which is much subtler, and this is the practice of mysticism. In every religion, mysticism represents the effort, as we said earlier, to seek an unmediated access to the divine presence and power. By its very nature, mysticism threatens the ordinary structures of sacred mediation. The mystic puts most emphasis upon prayer and meditation, on an inner journey. Therefore, the mystic tends to be individualistic rather than communal. The mystic insists on the superiority of the internal over the external, on the spirit over the physical. To put it very crudely, the mystics continue the tradition of Gnosticism, within the larger church. Therefore, they by their very nature are an ambivalent phenomenon within an exoteric tradition. There have always been Christian mystics, however.

Jesus himself was undoubtedly a mystic, somebody who had visions of his relationship with God as Father. We see this in the Gospels, in the baptism, and in the transfiguration of Jesus. Paul was a mystic, encountered the risen Lord in a vision on the road to Damascus, and in I Corinthians chapter 12, verses 1 to 5, talks about ascending into the third heaven.

There have been mystics throughout the history of Christianity: In the 12th and 13th centuries, as I said, Francis of Assisi had such a mystical identification with Jesus that he bore the marks of Jesus in his body; the 14th century mystics, especially the great English mystics and the mystics of the Rhineland, people like Meister Eckhart, and Hildegard of Bignen; and in the 16th century, the great Spanish mystics, Theresa of Avila and John of the Cross.

The Christian tradition has a rich collection of mystical literature that shows an inner path of seeking unity with Christ that does not deny the external tradition, but rather sees it as inadequate for the full realization of the spiritual life.

These radical forms of Christianity have often served as catalysts for reform. They challenge the conventions. They provide an opportunity for excellence. They also, of course, as so often happens, provide an occasion for elitism, that the only real Christians are the heroic Christians. Those who marry, raise a family, and so forth—those who are lay people—are not quite as much Christian as those who have poverty, obedience, and virginity. Often, they serve as the causes of division. The prophet, the reformer, and the mystic— these people challenge the community. Sometimes, however, they have also caused it to divide more fundamentally. We'll pursue that thought more in a further presentation.

Catholic, Orthodox, Protestant
Lecture 9

> This is one of the paradoxes of the Christian religion; it is a religion that
> has had unity as an ideal, and yet throughout its history has experienced
> conflict and division.

The ideal of unity is expressed in the New Testament and is stated by the creed as one of the four "marks of the church." The early centuries were marked by a variety of severe conflicts concerning belief and practice: The New Testament shows sharp disagreements between Christian groups (see Galatians, 2 and 3 John); the 2nd century struggle for self-definition involved sharp ideological and political divisions; and the battles involving Trinitarian and Christological doctrine in the 4th and 5th centuries likewise had ecclesiastical and political overtones. The three great families in Christianity arose from specific contentious circumstances between the 11th and 16th centuries and led to three distinct and usually competing versions of the religion. Each of them claims to best represent the essence of Christianity. Each of them claims a particular kind of continuity with Christian origins. All of them share the same basic story, creed, and moral teaching but differ most on questions of organization, theological emphasis, and worship.

The Roman Catholic tradition claims simply to be "catholic" but the designation *Roman* signifies what distinguishes it from Orthodoxy and Protestantism. Catholics share the basic elements sketched in earlier lectures and regard them as essential to its claim of a continuous tradition reaching back to the Apostle Peter. The organization of the church is universal and hierarchical, with authority coming from the Bishop of Rome (the pope), through archbishops and bishops, to the local clergy and laity of dioceses throughout the world. The Catholic clergy is all male, is celibate, and has a sacramental focus. The ministry of local parish priests is supplemented by that of active religious orders, such as the Jesuits and Dominicans. Catholicism claims and cultivates a powerful intellectual tradition reaching from Augustine and other patristic authors, through Aquinas and other Scholastic masters, to contemporary philosophers and theologians. The sacramental piety of Catholicism extends to devotion to the "communion of saints," among whom Mary, the Mother of Jesus, receives most attention.

The Orthodox tradition also claims continuity with the earliest church. Indeed, the embrace of "holy tradition" (*hagia paradosis*) is emphatic in a version of Christianity that eschews change. Orthodoxy shares most with Catholicism. The two camps split as a result of schism in 1054, the climax of centuries of growing tension between the old Rome and the "New Rome" of Constantinople. Political rivalry between capitals was expressed by religious rivalry between patriarchates, and the Latin-speaking West (facing the rapid changes subsequent on barbarian invasions) grew culturally apart from the more stable Greek-speaking East. Specific causes of schism involved diplomatic misunderstandings and the theological dustup around the phrase "and the Son" (*filioque*) in the creed.

The Orthodox tradition is dominant in Greece, Russia, the Slavic nations, Turkey, Cyprus, and the Middle East. Organization is patriarchal, with special honor given to the Patriarch of Constantinople. Local clergy are married, but the long-standing monastic tradition is celibate, and bishops are drawn from among monks. Orthodox spirituality is rich and complex, with particular emphasis on an apophatic mysticism. The veneration of the saints is reflected in the use of icons in liturgy and in contemplative prayer. The resistance to the iconoclastic movement within Orthodoxy (influenced by Islam) was a defining moment in shaping this tradition's character. Orthodoxy is centered in worship.

Martin Luther (1483–1546), German theologian and religious reformer.

The liturgy is regarded as a participation in the heavenly worship and is a powerfully moving and transforming experience.

The Protestant tradition began in the 16th century as an attempt to reform what was regarded as the corrupt Catholicism of the late-medieval period. Although symbolically connected to the figure of Martin Luther and John Calvin, the Reformation took many forms from the beginning and has developed in distinct ways. The overall feature that most distinguishes Protestantism from Catholicism and Orthodoxy is its emphasis on verbal revelation, preaching, and Scripture. The Lutheran tradition emphasized a return to Scripture as the norm for Christian life and a concentration on faith as the means of being in right relationship with God. It is found especially among Germanic and Nordic populations.

The Anglican tradition began as a schismatic break with Rome by King Henry VIII but, under Thomas Cranmer, developed a distinctive reform of the Catholic tradition, reflected above all, in the forms of piety found in the *Book of Common Prayer*. Anglicans (or Anglo-Catholics, or Episcopalians) are primarily English speaking. This tradition uses both ancient tradition and reason in its reading of Scripture and is, therefore, characterized by a highly intellectual character.

In the 18th century, Methodism began as a lay reform movement within Anglicanism that emphasized fervent piety in imitation of the ancient monks. Methodists, in addition to Scripture, tradition, and reason as norms for their lives, add, revealingly, experience. The Methodist (or Wesleyan) tradition places a high premium on experience and the transformation of the heart.

The Reformed tradition began in France and Switzerland with John Calvin but achieved great success among English-speaking populations under John Knox. Strict and intellectually rigorous, the Presbyterian tradition embraces the doctrine of predestination and elicits an enthusiastic commitment to good works.

The Anabaptist (meaning, "to be baptized again") movement in 16th-century Germany emphasized free and intentional commitment reflected in the practice of adult baptism. It broke away from the centralized, hierarchical tradition of other sects and is centered in the local congregation, each local congregation being freestanding. The Baptists represent the largest (and most "evangelical") form of Protestantism worldwide; most Baptists reject any form of creed or hierarchy and put tremendous emphasis on liberty. There are literally thousands of other versions of Protestantism, including Holiness and Pentecostal traditions, and a spectrum of local or national amalgamations of the dominant traditions.

The biggest scandal to non-Christians in this constant proliferation of Christian denominations is the intense rivalry and hostility that has so often existed among them, deriving from each one's claim to be the exclusive representative of authentic Christianity (see final lecture). ■

Suggested Reading

J. L. McKenzie, *The Roman Catholic Church* (New York: Holt, Rinehart and Winston, 1969).

M. E. Marty, *Protestantism* (New York: Holt, Rinehart and Winston, 1972).

A. Schmemann, *The Historical Road of Eastern Orthodoxy*, translated by L.W. Kesich (New York: Holt, Rinehart and Winston, 1963).

Questions to Consider

1. Comment on this proposition: "The differences among Catholic, Orthodox, and Protestant Christians are less doctrinal and moral than they are cultural."

2. How does each family in Christianity make a claim to represent "the origins" and "the essence" of the Christian religion?

Catholic, Orthodox, Protestant
Lecture 9—Transcript

In the previous lectures, I have tried to give some sense of Christianity as a religion, presenting pretty much the ideal form of this religion, talking about its story, its creed, its forms of worship, its moral teaching, and in the last presentation—its radical expressions.

In these last four lectures of this course, I want to complicate the picture a little bit by showing some of the varieties within the Christian tradition and its complex interactions with politics and with culture.

In this presentation, I begin with the obvious that when we look around in the world today, we find Christians coming in three major varieties—the Catholic, the Protestant, and the Orthodox—with many other sub-varieties. These different kinds of Christians don't often like each other very much.

This is one of the paradoxes of the Christian religion; it is a religion that has had unity as an ideal, and yet throughout its history has experienced conflict and division.

The ideal of unity is expressed in the New Testament. John has Jesus himself praying at his Last Supper with his disciples, that they may all be one. In his letter to the Ephesians, chapter 4, verse 4, Paul the Apostle says that there is one body, one spirit, one hope, one love, one faith, one baptism, one God and Father of all.

The Nicene Creed states, as one of the essential marks of the church, together with its being Catholic, Apostolic, and holy, that it be one.

Nevertheless, even the early centuries of the church were marked by a variety of severe conflicts concerning belief and practice.

Already in the New Testament, we see that in Paul's letter to the Galatians, he opposes those who want to impose circumcision on Gentile believers, and advocates their being expelled from the community.

In the first and second letters of John, we see that there is a process of mutual excommunication going on in those communities over the proper or improper understanding of who Jesus really is.

We have seen also in the second century that the major conflict with Gnosticism that resulted in Christianity's self definition as a public and exoteric tradition, involves severe ideological conflicts over the value of the body, as well as ecclesiastical politics concerning the significance and the value of a visible organized community.

Those long dreary Christological and Trinitarian battles of the fourth and fifth centuries involved ecclesiastical and political dimensions as well, particularly between the churches of Alexandria and Antioch, where bishops had developed separate theological traditions, separate understandings of who God was, and who Christ was, while sharing the basic frame of that belief, but nevertheless giving it different nuance, and different emphasis. There was also a dimension of political rivalry between those great cities and between the Christian communities in those cities. Thus, Christianity has never been without division, never been without conflict, despite its commitment to unity.

The three great families of Christians in the world today arose from specific contentious circumstances between the 11th and the 16th centuries of the C.E. They developed into three distinct and often, perhaps even usually, competing versions of this religion. Each of them claims to represent the essence of Christianity; if Christianity is the one true religion, this version is the truest of the one true religion.

Each of them claims a particular kind of continuity with Christian origins. In the case of Roman Catholicism, it claims a direct institutional continuity with the first Apostles. In the case of the Orthodox tradition, there is the claim to a continuous and unchanging tradition of teaching. In the case of Protestantism, it is the claim to have recovered the original essence and enthusiasm and spirit of Christianity found in the New Testament church.

For the most part, all three of these families share those elements of Christianity that I sketched in my opening lectures. They basically share the same story, the same creed, and the same moral teaching. They differ most on questions of organization, theological emphasis, and worship.

In this presentation, I want to review the three traditions and sketch what the salient elements are for purposes of instant recognition with regard to each of them.

The Roman Catholic tradition claims simply to be catholic, that is, universal, embracing everything. The designation of "Roman" signifies what distinguishes it from Orthodoxy and Protestantism. Roman Catholics are the most numerous Christians worldwide, with over one billion adherents throughout the world; that is, over half of all Christians are Roman Catholics. Even in North America, which is usually thought of as a Protestant country, Catholics outnumber Protestants, 71.4 million to 70.1 million. Catholics share the basic elements that I have sketched in the earlier lectures, and regard them as essential to its claim of a continuous tradition, reaching back to the Apostle Peter. Thus, the Bishop of Rome, called the Pope, claims to be the direct descendant, obviously not biological but through institutional descent, of the Apostle Peter, the first Bishop of Rome according to tradition. Indeed, the Roman Catholic Church is the oldest continuous public institution in the Western world.

The organization of the Roman Catholic Church is universal, in that there is a single, organizational web throughout the world. It is centralized in the city of Rome, in the Vatican, which is the residence of the Bishop of Rome, the Pope.

It is hierarchical. That is, authority moves downward from the Bishop of Rome to archbishops and bishops who govern individual dioceses. The word "diocese" describes the geographical area over which a bishop governs, and the bishops in turn are in charge of the clergy and the priesthood in that particular area.

In Roman Catholic understanding, the teaching and governing authority is distinguished between the "ordinary magisterium" authority, and the "extraordinary magisterium."

The "ordinary magisterium," or teaching office of the church, is located in the bishops, in their collectivity.

"Extraordinary magisterium" is the distinctive authority ascribed to the Bishop of Rome, to the Pope. This is particularly true when he speaks, as it is said, *Ex cathedra*, that is, from his official position on matters of faith and morals, in which cases Roman Catholics regard the teaching of the Bishop of Rome as infallible, and as guaranteed true.

The Catholic clergy are all male, are celibate, and have a sacramental focus. The focus is particularly on the celebration of the Eucharist. The ministry of local priests is supplemented by that of active religious orders, both male and female, such as the Society of Jesus, otherwise known as the Jesuits, or the Order of Preachers, known as the Dominicans, or the Franciscans, the mendicant orders.

There are also a variety of monastic orders, such as the Benedictans, the Carthusians, the Cistercians, and so forth, both male and female, obviously separately; they live celibate lives. In addition to some of them being contemplative in this mission, others are active and perform a wide variety of ministries, including medicine and education.

The Catholic tradition claims and cultivates a powerful intellectual heritage. It must be said that it is located particularly in the Benedictine monastic tradition, in the Society of Jesus, and the Order of Preachers; it reaches from Saint Augustine and other patristic authors through Thomas Aquinas—the great theologian of the 13th century—and other Scholastic masters, to contemporary philosophers. These include Jacque Murray, Gabriel Marcel, and theologians like the great Karl Rahner, and a contemporary Catholic theologian, Hans Urs von Balthasar.

If one wants to make a quick and ready contrast between Catholicism and Protestantism, it would be in the focus on the sacraments, on those seven ritual activities that I described in an earlier lecture. The sacramental piety of Catholicism extends to a devotion to the Communion of Saints. Indeed, many Catholics think of having a patron saint, or a particular saint to whom that person is devoted.

For all Catholics, particular devotion is given to the mother of Jesus, Mary. A very popular Catholic devotion is the prayer called the Rosary, which consists of a series of prayers spelled off on beads. This is a prayer called the "Hail Mary," and is largely derived from Scripture. It is accompanied by meditations on the Gospel narratives.

The Rosary, in fact, within Catholicism, is not dissimilar to the prayer beads of Muslims who tick off the many names of Allah. In fact, there may have been a historical connection between the development of the Rosary, and the prayer beads of Islam.

Let me say a few words about the Orthodox tradition. It is numerically smallest; there are about 216 million members of the Orthodox tradition worldwide in several different linguistic and ethnic divisions. There are about four million of the Orthodox persuasion in the United States of America. The Orthodox tradition also claims direct continuity with the earliest church, and it does this through the explicit and enthusiastic embrace of what it calls *hagia paradosis*, the "holy or sacred tradition."

In this version of Christianity, there is a positive rejection of change; there is a cultivation of continuity. One has little sense in Orthodoxy of any particular significance given to historical, technological, cultural, intellectual change. It bypasses all of the upheavals that were found in Europe through the Renaissance, the Reformation, and the Revolution and industrial development.

In terms of its religious focus, Orthodoxy shares most with Catholicism; it has the same kind of sacramental focus, same kind of appreciation of antiquity, and so forth. The two camps split as a result of what is called a "schism," a formal split, in the year 1054, in the 11ᵗʰ century. However, this had been preceded by centuries of growing tension between the old Rome, and the "New Rome" of Constantinople that had been founded by Constantine as the new imperial center in the East.

The political rivalry between old Rome and "New Rome" was accompanied by religious rivalry between the patriarch of Rome, the Pope, the patriarch of Constantinople, and the Latin-speaking West, which faced the rapid cataclysmic changes subsequent upon the dissolution of the Imperial Order, the incursion of barbarian invasions, and the unchanging Greek-speaking culture of Constantinople in what is called the Byzantine Empire. The Empire of the East, centered in Constantinople, continued in its Greek-speaking culture, unchanging until the 16ᵗʰ century, when Byzantium was finally conquered by Islam.

By contrast, in the West, the barbarian king Charles the Great Charlemagne was crowned the new Emperor of the Holy Roman Empire by the Pope. This had very little to do with Rome indeed, except that Charlemagne was crowned by the Pope.

The specific clauses of the schism involved diplomatic misunderstandings between these two camps, and the theological dustup around what appears to be a very trivial phrase. The phrase in Latin is *filioque*, "and the Son." It was inserted in the court of Charlemagne into the Creed that was recited by Christians. The traditional Nicene Creed had simply, concerning the Holy Spirit, said that the Holy Spirit was to be worshipped and glorified with the Father and the Son, and proceeds from the Father. The West thought that was a little inadequate, and they added "and the Son." This affronted the tradition-affirming group in the East. That tiny phrase was the straw that broke the camel's back, after these centuries of cultural linguistic misunderstanding.

The East basically said the West was wrong, and it affirmed the ancient and continuous tradition. It said that the West was innovative, stupid, and barbarian, basically. That schism over such a tiny point has fundamentally never been resolved, and of course it grew greater as the cultural differences between the Greek East and the Latin West grew ever deeper.

The Orthodox tradition remains dominant in Greece, Russia, the Slavic nations, Turkey, Cyprus, and the Middle East. The organization of the Orthodox community is patriarchal and hierarchical, with special honor given to the Bishop of Constantinople, I should say the patriarch of Constantinople.

Local clergy in the Orthodox communion are male, but are married. The longstanding monastic tradition within Orthodoxy is celibacy, and bishops within the Orthodox tradition tend to be selected either from the celibate monks, or from those ordinary priests who choose to remain celibate. Thus, Orthodox bishops are celibate, but local clergy are usually married.

Orthodox spirituality is rich and complex, with particular emphasis on what is called the apophatic tradition of mysticism. Especially among monks, there developed a profound sense of mysticism connected with the prayer of silence, sometimes called "Hesychasm," from the Greek word *hesychios*, which means "silence."

Another dimension of this mystical tradition is the veneration of the saints through the use of icons. The word "icon" comes from the Greek *eikon*, which means "image." Very early on in the Orthodox tradition, there grew the custom of portraying the saints, or Jesus, or Mary, or scenes from Jesus's life, in terms of exquisite pictorial representation. These were really thought to be revelatory; they were objects of contemplation and prayer. They have currently become very popular in the West as *objet d'art*. You can scarcely walk into a gift shop without finding icons on sale, but it's very important to remember that for Orthodox, this is not art. It is, rather, a form of religious expression.

Indeed, the Orthodox resistance to the icono-classic movement within Orthodoxy, breaking of icons, where that tradition of silence and Hesychasm came into conflict with the popular piety of pictures and representations and was deeply influenced by the way Islam viewed its images. This controversy occurred in the eighth century when Islam was on the rise. Islam, of course, destroys all images and refuses to give any pictorial representation to Allah.

The Orthodox resistance to iconoclasm was really a defining moment in this tradition. Orthodoxy is centered in worship. The liturgy is regarded as a participation in heavenly worship taking place now, and is a physically demanding, powerfully moving, and transforming experience.

The Protestant tradition began in the 16th century, although it actually climaxed a series of reforms that had begun already in the previous century, as an attempt to reform what was regarded as the corrupt Catholicism of the late Medieval period.

Catholicism had, I think everybody would agree, lost touch with the essence of the religion. It had become too hierarchical, too legalistic, and too morally corrupt, and reform was needed.

Although symbolically connected to the name of Martin Luther in Germany, and John Calvin in France and Switzerland, the Reformation took many forms from the beginning, and has developed in distinctive ways. I can say very briefly that in all forms of the Reformation, the clergy are married and very often female. Protestantism occurs in a variety of organizational forms, from the use of bishops to democratically elected leaders at the local level.

Overall, however, Protestantism has traditionally placed a much greater emphasis upon the ministry of preaching than on the sacraments, so there is much more emphasis upon the verbal character of revelation, and therefore of Scripture and scriptural preaching, than one finds in Catholicism or in Orthodoxy.

Here's a very brief and terribly unfair review of some of the major elements. The Lutheran tradition, beginning with Martin Luther, emphasized a return to Scripture. Luther's phrase was *sola scriptura*, "scripture alone," as the norm for Christian life, and a concentration on faith. Luther's slogan was *sola fides*, "faith alone," as the means of being in right relationship with God. These slogans set themselves against the developments that had happened in Catholicism over the centuries, and represent a return to simplicity, a willingness to go back to the origins in Scripture and to what was regarded as the essential feature of Christianity, which was the response of the heart to God, rather than the observance of thousands and thousands of particular kinds of observances decreed by the church. The Lutheran tradition is found particularly in the Germanic and Nordic populations. In the United States today there are about eight million Lutherans.

The Anglican tradition began as a schismatic break with Rome by King Henry the VIII. You will remember that there was a marriage and divorce involved in all of this, and Henry the VIII paradoxically had been declared by the Pope a defender of the faith, because he had opposed the reformation in Germany on the side of Catholicism. Out of his desire for an heir, however, Henry sought dissolution of his first marriage; this was rejected, and Henry the VIII found a way.

Under Thomas Cranmer, the Anglican Church, the Church of England, developed a distinctive reform of the Catholic tradition, reflected above all in the forms of piety found in what is known as the *Book of Common Prayer*, which is by everybody's estimation one of the masterpieces of English prose.

The Anglo-Catholic tradition, or Episcopalian tradition, is primarily English-speaking; in the United States, there are about 2.3 million members of the Anglo-Catholic or Episcopalian tradition. The Episcopal tradition looks not only to Scripture, but also to the tradition and to the use of reason in using Scripture. Therefore, it is often characterized by a high intellectual character.

The tradition called Methodism began in the 18th century under Oxford students, the brothers John and Charles Wesley; they wanted to reform Anglicanism by emphasizing fervent piety, expressed above all in the marvelous hymns composed by Charles Wesley, and the practices, therefore the method, of piety.

The practices of piety were paradoxically in imitation of the ancient monks, but were now carried out by lay people who committed themselves as disciples to groups who would try to lead fervent lives. Methodists, in addition to Scripture and tradition and reason as norms for their lives, add, revealingly, experience. It is a tradition that places a very high premium on personal experience and on the transformation of the heart. There are about

12 million members of the Methodist or—as it also sometimes is called—the "Wesleyan" tradition in the United States of America.

The Reformed tradition began in France and Switzerland with John Calvin, but achieved great success among English-speaking populations under John Knox in Scotland.

This Reform tradition, also sometimes called the Presbyterian tradition, is strict and intellectually rigorous. The great 20th century theologian Karl Bart, for example, is a member of the Reformed tradition. The Presbyterian tradition embraces the doctrine of election by grace, has an elected leadership, and elicits an enthusiastic commitment to good works. It is also quite small; there are about five million members of the Presbyterian community in the United States of America.

Next, there are Christians who belong to the broad Anabaptist tradition. The Anabaptists began in Germany about the same time that the Lutheran tradition did, but it was a much more radical form of reformation. Lutheranism remained very closely identified with Catholicism, and really was a sort of corrective to Catholicism. It retained many elements of the sacraments and so forth, with an emphasis upon Scripture and faith.

The Anabaptist tradition privileged what might be called the independent status of the individual congregation. It broke more decisively away from the hierarchical centralized organization of other traditions. Thus, each congregation is "free-standing," and there's a strong emphasis upon adult conversion, thus "Ana-baptist," to be baptized again, the practice of adult baptism. It is centered, as I said, in the local congregation, and is sometimes called the Free Church tradition.

This is the largest form of Protestantism today, especially in the United States, and it is the most evangelical, and the most explicitly Scripturally based. Most Baptists reject any form of creed, any form of hierarchy, and really put a tremendous emphasis upon the liberty of Christians.

There are about 29 million Baptists in the United States, and it is growing rapidly, especially in Eastern Europe. It is by far the largest group of Protestants in the United States.

Finally, there are literally thousands of other versions of Protestantism, including the Holiness traditions, Pentecostal traditions, and a spectrum of national and local amalgams of all of these kinds of traditions. There really is a bewildering variety of forms of Christianity on offer today, many of them simply springing up from the ground because some local Christian regards himself or herself as having a special calling; she or he begins a congregation, and out of that grows a kind of a loose network of affiliation.

The biggest scandal to non-Christians in this constant splintering and proliferation of Christian denominations is the intense rivalry and hostility that has so often existed among them, deriving from each one's claim to be an exclusive representation of authentic Christianity. Diversity in itself is by no means a scandalous proposition. Indeed, it might be a source of rich resources within the Christian tradition and the variety of styles of expressing certain shared beliefs and practices.

It is the exclusivity of these claims, however, that is shocking to those who see Christianity proclaiming unity and not practicing it. Whether it is the Bishop of Rome who governs over a billion Christians worldwide—or the pastor of a local church in Decatur, Georgia, who is preaching to 50 people—there is something ludicrous in the claim to being the only absolute representation of the truth. When Christian diversity becomes division, and when it becomes rivalry, it becomes a weakness to Christianity, and weakens Christianity's claim to be taken seriously very severely.

Christianity and Politics
Lecture 10

For much of its existence, [Christianity] has been deeply involved in politics and in culture.

One reason that Christianity is so seldom appreciated in strictly religious terms is that, for much of its existence, it has been deeply involved in politics and culture. This is one of Christianity's many paradoxes, because it began life as a sect of Judaism that met resistance and persecution. Jesus was executed by Roman authority as a messianic pretender. Paul and other first-generation leaders were repeatedly imprisoned. The tradition of martyrdom and of apologetic literature through Christianity's first centuries testify to its political powerlessness.

Christianity's initial focus—found in the New Testament—was on the shaping of an intentional community. It was ill-equipped to become the imperial religion. In this respect, Christianity is distinct both from Judaism and Islam, whose systems of law had the shaping of a society in view from the beginning. Remember the complexity of Christian moral teaching in the New Testament, and think of using the New Testament to guide the religious life of a civilization.

In 313, the Emperor Constantine converted and established Christianity as the official religion of the Roman Empire; the "Constantinian era" has affected Christianity up to the present. The motivations of the emperor were undoubtedly complex and, at least in part, involved the recognition that Christianity had grown too powerful to suppress; as Tertullian had declared, "the blood of the martyrs is the seed of the Church." Constantine's summoning of the Council of Nicea in 325 indicated the need to have a unified Christianity as the glue of society. Under Theodosius I, the establishment of Christianity was complete, and both Judaism and Greco-Roman religions became severely disadvantaged.

In the East, the Constantinian connection took the form of Caesaro-Papism, in which there was a close cooperation between political and ecclesiastical authorities. Such emperors as Leo and Justinian considered themselves

Credit Doré's Illustrations of the Crusades; Courtesy of Dover Pictorial Archive Series.

King Richard I (also known as Richard the Lionheart) of England led battles during the Third Crusade. His military prowess earned him his sobriquet.

theologians, as well as leaders of the state. The "New Rome" held off the "infidels" (Muslims) for centuries in the name of Christ, until the final conquest of Constantinople in 1516. In the West, the ascendancy of the pope made for a sharper distinction between political and religious authority, but the history of "Christendom" was one in which both popes and kings thought of themselves as servants of God.

The four crusades undertaken by European Christians to retake the Holy Land from Muslims represented the ideal of state/church collaboration. We should note several paradoxes of these crusades. Christians, who in the beginning, proclaimed only a new heavenly Jerusalem and awaited the coming again of Jesus, were now involved in a real estate and trade venture, in conquering the Holy Land as a political and religious acquisition. The last and fourth crusade ended with Christian warriors sacking the city of Constantinople, which was

The American, French, and Russian Revolutions each called into question the place of Christianity as a state religion.

a Christian city! Christians today who are upset by the concept of Islamic *jihad* should remember that the notion of a holy war (a crusade) is deeply ingrained in the Christian tradition.

Equally a manifestation of the Constantinian outlook is the Inquisition, a cooperative effort between the church and the state to establish uniformity. It tortured and sometimes killed heretics (and Jews), both for the sake of the church and the "Christian state"—to keep them pure.

The expulsion of Jews from Spain in 1492 is another example of the profound affiliation of politics and religion in medieval Europe. Even with the Reformation, the same assumed link between political and religious power continued on every side: In European countries, the principle of *cuius regio, eius religio* ("whoever is prince, his is the religion") divided a continent into Catholic and Protestant countries that entered into long-lasting religious wars. World exploration by European adventurers served the ends of ecclesiastical, as well as political, desires. A divided Christianity was transported to new lands, as mission and colonialism merged in a competition for souls and the importation of European culture as "Christian."

Since the 18th century, the Constantinian era has been challenged above all in the West through political revolutions. The American, French, and Russian Revolutions each called into question the place of Christianity as a state religion. In the United States, the "separation of church and state" removes the privilege of establishment without directly attacking Christianity or any other religion. In France, a more aggressive revolt against the church in the name of secular ideals (that themselves took on religious coloration) continued the old struggle over property and power. The Bolshevik Revolution in Russia took its stand on the explicit repudiation of, and systematic attempt to eradicate, all religion.

Christians today struggle to come to grips with the reversal in the religion's political fortunes. Some Christians still consider the Constantinian arrangement the ideal and seek to assert Christian political power. Others rejoice in the separation of the religion from political power and see it as a chance to recover some of the essential dimensions of the religion that its long political history tended to obscure. ■

Essential Reading

Eusebius of Caesarea, *Life of Constantine*, translation and commentary by A. Cameron and S. G. Hall (Oxford: Clarendon Press, 1999).

Supplemental Reading

J. Carroll, *Constantine's Sword: The Church and the Jews: A History* (Boston: Houghton Mifflin, 2001).

T. Parker, *Christianity and the State in the Light of History* (London: A&C Black, 1955).

J. Pelikan, *The Excellent Empire: The Fall of Rome and the Triumph of the Church* (San Francisco: HarperSanFrancisco, 1987).

1. Did becoming the imperial religion change Christianity superficially or fundamentally?

2. How has Christianity's place in the world been altered by the intellectual and political challenges since the 17th century?

Christianity and Politics
Lecture 10—Transcript

In the last presentation, we saw how Christianity, despite its ideal of unity, has from the beginning experienced internal dissention, and now appears in the early 21st century in an almost bewildering variety of groups. These groups not only differ on many points, but until very recently were positively hostile to each other, each claiming exclusive possession of the truth.

In this presentation, I want to examination another paradox of the Christian religion, a tradition that proclaimed a crucified Messiah who gave power to others through powerlessness. It is a tradition that proclaimed a Messiah who was the Prince of Peace that found itself enmeshed in patterns of power, politics, and even of violence over its long history.

Our topic in this presentation is Christianity in the World: Religion and Politics. This is one reason why Christianity is so difficult to appreciate in strictly religious terms. For much of its existence, it has been deeply involved in politics and in culture, and this is one of many of Christianity's paradoxes.

It began life as a sect of Judaism that itself met resistance and persecution. Jesus was a Jewish preacher who was executed under Roman authority, Pontius Pilate the Prefect of Palestine, as a messianic pretender, that is, as a politic figure. The *titilus*, the title on the cross, read "Jesus of Nazareth, King of the Jews." Thus, at least in the eyes of Rome, one of the problems with Jesus was that he was meddling in politics.

Paul was himself, earlier in his life, a persecutor of this early Christian movement, and was himself imprisoned repeatedly under Roman authority; he was finally executed. Indeed, by the year 70, virtually all the major leaders of the movement had met a violent end at the hands of Rome. Throughout the first three centuries of Christianity, the tradition of martyrdom, and the tradition of writing apologetic literature, testifies to its politic powerlessness, and to the fact that the political order found it dangerous and needing extirpation.

As I tried to show in an earlier lecture on Christian morality, this minority and persecuted status of early Christianity ill prepared it to become the religion of an empire. This is in sharp contrast to both Judaism and Islam. In Judaism, Torah was, from the beginning, intended to shape a society, Jewish society. Likewise, in Islam the Shahariah was intended from the beginning to create an entire society governed under the prophet's revelation of the will of Allah.

Christians, from the beginning, had no concern except the shaping of their tiny and persecuted communities. Their horizons hardly even were raised to the level of the household in terms of ethics, and they had no vision of how society should be run as a whole. If we look at the New Testament, and simply look at what the New Testament recommends in terms of an attitude towards the Roman Empire, we see that in Romans 13 and in I Peter 3, the Roman Empire is regarded in entirely positive terms: Everybody should obey the emperor because the emperor is a good guy. If we look at the Book of Revelation, however, we see that the Empire is regarded as a destructive and enslaving force that Christians should resist by their worship of the only king of kings, who is Jesus Christ. The New Testament is not a guidebook for the running of a Christian civilization.

Thus, when we come to the year 313, which is the great divide in the history of Christianity, when Constantine converted to the Christian religion and established Christianity as the official religion of the Roman Empire through the Edict of Milan and began what is called the Constantine era, Christianity underwent fundamental changes.

The motivations of Constantine himself were undoubtedly mixed. The church writer and historian Eusebius, in his laudatory, if not fawning biography of the Emperor Constantine, *Vita Constantini*, describes this conversion to Christianity as a result of a revelation that Constantine had in battle at the Milvian bridge, where he saw a vision of heaven and of the cross of Jesus. Under it, *in hoc vigno vinces*, "in this sign you will conquer."

You see the sort of mixed motivation already involved that. This is a pretty good sign with which to go to battle. That sign of the cross became for

Constantine, then, the center for his organization of the Empire. Whatever his motivation, it at least involved in part the recognition that Christianity had grown by this time too numerous to completely suppress. Already in the third century, Tertullian had said that the blood of martyrs was the seed of the church. Christianity seemed to be the sort of movement that, the more you tried to repress it and suppress it, the more it simply grew. Therefore, Christians had become sufficiently populous in the Empire that, according to many historians, Constantine made the prudential judgment of "If you can't beat them, then join them," and that it was better to align himself with the Christian religion than with what was clearly a sort of fading Greco-Roman religion or paganism.

For all emperors, it is very important that religion be the glue of the Empire. Constantine was no exception. One of the very first things that Constantine did was call the Counsel of Nicea in the year 325. He summoned all of the Christian bishops to meet in the city of Nicea to settle their doctrinal disputes; these disputes had been generated by the Alexandrian priest, Arius. This led them to the development of the Nicene Creed that we talked about in an earlier presentation; it was this formal statement of belief to which all Christian bishops were to adhere. If they didn't, they should leave the Empire.

As we saw, what happened then is that official orthodox Christianity was really the imperial religion and heterodox or divergent forms of Christianity tended to be able to thrive only outside of the imperial reach in North Africa and in East Syria.

The establishment of Christianity did not happen totally under Constantine or his immediate successors. Indeed, in the 360s a person whom Christians called Julian the Apostate, the Emperor Julian, tried to turn the Empire back to paganism. He died very young in battle, and his experiment failed. His successor, Theodosius I, finally succeeded in effectively establishing Christianity as the official religion of the Empire in the late fourth century.

It is very important to note that with the establishment of Christianity also began the history of Christian intolerance for any other religious tradition. Immediately, under Theodosius, things got very rough for Jews and for pagans so that the ancient Greco-Roman religious temples, statues, and so forth were destroyed or expropriated. Christianity took itself seriously as a religion of the Empire or as an imperial religion.

Now in the Eastern empire, the Byzantine Empire, the Constantinian connection took the form of what is called Caesaro-Papism, "Caesar and the Pope," if you will, in a religious political nexus. In the East, there was always a very close cooperation between the religious authorities and the political authorities. Emperors like Leo I and Justinian considered themselves to be as much the head of the church as of the state. Indeed, both of them considered themselves to be—and were considered by others—as right good theologians.

The "New Rome" in Constantinople, the Byzantine kingdom, held the "infidels," the Muslims, at bay, protecting their diminished kingdom in Constantinople in the name of Christ until 1560. Until early in the 16th century, that imperial realm continued in direct continuity with Constantine, and with that very close connection between political and religious rule.

An indication of this is found even in the early 20th century with the close cooperation between Czarist Russia—notice Czar is a form of Caesar—and Russian Orthodoxy. Moscow claimed to be the third Rome; the successor of Constantinople as the center of Christianity. Thus, the Czar, the Russian ruler, was the new Caesar.

The patriarch of Moscow was the equivalent of the patriarch of Constantinople, and there was the development of this notion of Holy Russia, which is so marked in the fiction of Dostoevsky and Tolstoy and the music of Mussorgsky. It eventually ended in the tragic alliance between the Czarina Alexandra and the Russian orthodox monk Rasputin, immediately before the Russian Revolution in 1917.

In the West, the ascendancy of the Bishop of Rome, the Pope, made for a sharper distinction between political and religious authority. This was particularly the case because the Pope claimed to have been deeded political authority over the West by the Emperor Constantine. This is the famous "Donation of Constantine." It was an actual legal document, which purportedly Constantine had used to hand over political rule of the West to the Bishop of Rome, so that the popes claimed to actually be in charge of everything in the West. Therefore, Christendom—the distinctive name given to that cultural, political, religious amalgam which was the civilization of the West during all of this period—involved the authority of both popes and kings in an uneasy alliance.

Popes wanted to crown kings, but often kings would try to assert their own authority. The conflict we talked about in the last presentation between Henry VIII and the papacy would be one of the final examples of that. Henry VIII finally established the church in England so that he could have the same unity between church and politics in his own realm. Both popes and kings thought of themselves as servants of God. Indeed, there was a popular slogan that they represented the "two swords" that Peter spoke of in the Gospel when Jesus was arrested. Peter as reported in the Gospel said, "Master, we have two swords," as though they were going to resist Jesus's arrestors. Jesus responds, "It is enough. Put them away."

These two swords were claimed to be the Pope and the Emperor; both of them wielded political and military power, and they exercised it over a very real kingdom, which was Western Europe.

These were two examples of some of the consequences of what was called the Holy Roman Empire, but might be regarded as an unholy alliance. The four crusades were undertaken in the 11th century by European Christians to retake the Holy Land, the land of Palestine, from Muslims who were regarded as infidels, unbelievers. The figure of Muhammad was described almost as a demonic figure, Mahout. The Muslims were regarded by these European Christians as subhuman even though they represented, at that time, the highest cultural form achieved by anybody in the West. This was an example of a kind of papal and imperial cooperation in the West, church-state collaboration.

Note several paradoxes of these crusades. The first paradox is that Christians who had in the beginning had proclaimed only a "New Jerusalem" that was heavenly and awaited the coming of Jesus and a participation in the life of God, now were involved in a real estate and trade adventure, to be sure, in conquering the Holy Land as a political and religious acquisition.

The second paradox is that the last and fourth crusade ended with Christian warriors sacking the city of Constantinople, which was a Christian city. In other words, it was sort of like letting the dogs loose. All kinds of things happen.

The third paradox is that Christians today who find themselves terribly upset at Islamic Jihad or Holy War need to develop more extensive memories, and acknowledge the fact that the notion of a crusade of a holy war is very deeply engrained within Christian tradition.

A second and equally sad manifestation of the Constantinian outlook is the Inquisition, which later became known as the Holy Office. This was a cooperative effort between the state and the church to establish uniformity of doctrine and observance within the political realm; it used violence, even execution.

From the 13th century on, heretics were tortured, killed, in order to extirpate heresy, and keep the kingdom pure of heresy. This was obviously both for the sake of the church and for the state of the "Christian state." Again, the irony of calling these executions of the Spanish Inquisition, *auto de fe,* "act of faith," is too deep to require comment. Fourteen ninety-two was not only the year in which Columbus sailed the ocean blue, but it was also the year in which those most Catholic majesties, Ferdinand and Isabella, expelled all Jews from Spain. This is an example of the kind of mixture of politics and of religion which became so enmeshed that it was very difficult for people to discern where one left off and the other started.

Unfortunately, this combination of Christian intolerance and political force did not cease with the Protestant Reformation. Even with the Reformation in Europe, the same premise that there should be a link between political and religious power continued on every side. John Calvin oversaw and approved the execution of a heretic in the city of Geneva. Martin Luther advocated the suppression by violence not only of Jews, the burning of the

Talmud, expulsion, and so forth, but also the suppression of the Anabaptist movement, the Radical Reformation. He wrote a notoriously virulent to the German princes; he scolded them for not using their might in order to suppress these forms of reformation, which were regarded as unseemly by the hero of Wittenberg.

Indeed, in European countries, the unified Latin culture began to disintegrate in the 16th century with world exploration on the one hand, but also with the development of individual principates and kingdoms. Individual European languages began to splinter off from Latin and the emergence of the Germanic languages contributed to the fragmentation of the old European unity of empire and church.

There developed the principle called *cuius regio, eius religio,* "whoever is prince, his is the religion". If the prince of Dutchie in Germany was Lutheran, then that kingdom was Lutheran. If the King of Spain was Catholic, Spain was Catholic.

One consequence of this was that Christians then became as intolerant of each other, and as politically violent with each other as they had been intolerant of Jews, heretics, and Muslims in earlier generations. What resulted was centuries of religious rule. There were the wars between nations in Europe that continued over several hundred years all in the name of Christ, remarkably, and in the name of the single "right" version of Christianity.

What also happened as a result is that all of this fragmentation, rivalry, hostility, and warfare accompanied the period of world exploration. As explorers were heading out to conquer new lands for European rulers in North America, Latin America, Africa, and Asia, during this same period of time they also imported a fragmented Christianity. Latin America is predominantly Roman Catholic because it's largely Latin. It was largely settled by Spanish and Portuguese rulers. North America was for the most part Protestant because it was founded by English settlers primarily, and then was mostly populated in the earlier years by other Protestant adherents.

A divided Christianity was transported to new lands as missionary competition and colonialism went hand-in-hand in a competition for souls, and for the importation of European culture as Christian culture.

It is precisely this, and it's an extraordinarily important point to make, that was one of the things that gave rise to the Enlightenment in the late 17th and early 18th centuries. At least one of the factors at work in the development of what is called modernity, or the spirit of Enlightenment, was a sense of moral revulsion at this kind of deeply internecine and indeed fratricidal hostility between competing versions of Christianity. Each of which was willing to use a sword in order to establish its form of the truth.

Since the 18th century, the "Constantinian era" has been fractured and challenged above all, in the West, through political revolution. That assumed connection between Christianity and the state has been decisively severed since the 18th century. There are three important revolutions that need to be noted: The American Revolution in 1776, the French Revolution in 1789, and the Russian Revolution in 1917. Each of these called into question the place of Christianity as a state religion, and really began to move into the politically secular world that most of us now inhabit.

In the United States, there has been a "separation of church and state," which removes the privilege of Christianity as an established religion, but is very careful not to directly attack Christianity or any other sort of religious observance. Freedom of religion is one of the guaranteed rights under the American Constitution.

There was also this very nervous sense among the framers of the constitution that in the American experiment, the disastrous previous history of Europe should not be repeated. There ought to be a respect for religion, but there ought to be also what Jefferson called this "wall of separation" between religion and the state.

The revolution in France in 1789 was a much more violent affair. The American Revolution was engendered by English-speaking people who already belonged to a variety of versions of Protestantism, primarily. They each were very eager to have their own freedom to practice, and to be assured that no one of them assumed dominance.

France was Catholic, and the movement of revolution in France had a much more unified form of opposition. The French Revolution took its stand upon certain principles, such as "*liberte, egalite, fraternite*," meaning, "brotherhood, liberty, and equality." These themselves almost became religious in character, and really sought not a separation of church and state, but the overthrow of the church in the name of a secular state. In France, there was a much tenser kind of relationship between a stubborn Catholicism, and a more violent and reactionary form of *secularism*, which really has continued for a very long time.

Finally, the Bolshevik Revolution in Russia took its stand on an even more radical position, which is the repudiation of all religion. Obviously, the Bolshevik revolution was led by Lenin, who was a disciple of Karl Marx.

Karl Marx began his philosophical works by following Ludwig Feuerbach, by declaring that all religious belief is simply projection, is simply a form of alienation. There is no divine power. There is no transcendence. It is simply, if you will, wish fulfillment on the part of humans. Thus, Karl Marx assumed that one must begin with the critique of religion before beginning the critique of capital and the critique of economics. He said that we've left religion behind, and had shown that religion is an alienation of humans; it promises them pie in the sky, by and by, but keeps them from recognizing their true human condition. Now we need to look at economic structures, and how people are separated from the fruits of their own labor, and the vision, then, of a classless society.

All of this was precisely what Lenin tried to impose through the Bolshevik Revolution in 1917. The first step is to get rid of the Czar and the Russian Orthodox Church, to take over all of the church buildings as museums of the state, and to actively try to eradicate Christianity through a very long process of social pressure, and of the education of the young, who are schooled in atheism.

As a result of these cataclysmic political changes, Christians today struggle to come to grips with the reversal in its political fortunes. Some Christians, remarkably, still consider the Constantinian arrangement, the idea, and long for an assertion of Christian political power and a Christian culture.

As recently as the 1960's, it was possible to find Spanish Catholic theologians arguing that religious tolerance is against Catholic teaching. To be Catholic means to be intolerant of other traditions. In the United States, among evangelical Christians, we find movements such as the Christian Coalition, which has among its goals the establishment of genuine Christian values that are explicitly supported by political means.

Other Christians, in contrast, rejoice in the separation of religion from political power and see it as an opportunity, a chance for Christianity to recover some of the essential dimensions of this religion that its long political history tended to obscure. They hope that Christianity can recover some of its original counter-cultural posture and be less compromised by political power.

Christianity and Culture
Lecture 11

Christianity has certainly been shaped by each of these cultural engagements, but Christianity has also helped shape culture. Even Judaism and Islam look differently because of the experience of Christianity.

Another paradox of Christianity is that a religion whose origins were countercultural should find itself so entwined with culture over the course of its history. At the explicit level, the New Testament gives scant encouragement to a positive engagement with culture. The mysterious revelation in Christ is pitted against "the wisdom of the world," that is, philosophy. Continuing the aconic tradition of Israel, the New Testament pays little attention to beauty, pleasure, or human artistry. Yet the New Testament uses rhetoric and elements of Greek philosophy; the incarnation (God is revealed through the human body) is a basis for art; and the stories of the Old Testament provide a rich cultural resource. Already in the 2nd century, Christian apologists confidently appropriated Platonic philosophy and considered Christianity to be a philosophical school. By the beginning of the 3rd century, wealthier Christians were using both biblical and pagan themes in funerary art.

When Christianity becomes the imperial religion under Constantine, it appropriates many aspects of Greco-Roman culture, even as it explicitly rejects paganism. In the realm of thought, the development of Christian doctrine owes much to philosophy. The doctrinal disputes of the 4th and 5th centuries were fundamentally ontological in character. Philosophical language even enters into the Nicene Creed (the *homoousios*). Christian writers wrote poetry and hymns in honor of Christ that made use of classical forms. Just as the hierarchy paralleled the complex administration of the empire, so did the occupation of great public spaces encourage the development of art. Public worship became a great "liturgy" with dramatic movement and elaborate costuming. Pictorial adornment of space helped identify it as sacred (see the mosaics at Ravenna). The use of icons—both private and public—is the perfect artistic expression of belief in the incarnation and in the sanctification of humanity.

In medieval Europe, the term *Christendom* expresses the complete integration of the Christian religion and culture. In the world of learning, theology was the "Queen of the Sciences" in the university, and Scholasticism achieved a remarkable rapprochement between the gospel and Aristotle. The great medieval cathedrals that sprang up across Europe were exhibits for the Christian story in carving and in stained glass. The liturgy of the Eucharist was the cultural form of drama, and the Gregorian chant sung at the Mass and the Divine Office was both music and scriptural interpretation.

The Renaissance and the Reformation, each in its fashion, developed and diminished the Christian form of culture. The culture of the Renaissance is, on the surface, still recognizably Christian but with an even deeper recovery of Greco-Roman (and pagan) influence. In music, painting, and sculpture, Christian themes abound (see Palestrina, Michelangelo, Leonardo de Vinci). At the same time, there is a difference: Art serves the vanity of prince and pope; the ideal of the body is Greek rather than Christian; and the rebirth of Plato challenges the unified worldview of Scholasticism. Lorenzo Valla's demonstration that the "Donation of Constantine" was a forgery stimulated the development of critical historiography.

The Reformation rejected the extravagance of late-medieval Catholicism in favor of a simpler and more scriptural Christianity. The reformers returned to an aconic approach to the visual arts. Note the use of the cross in Protestant churches rather than the Crucifix. Yet see also the marvelous carvings, etchings, and paintings of the

Renaissance art is still Christian on the surface, but at a deeper level it represents the recovery of Greco-Roman influences, as seen in Michelangelo's *David*.

Reformation. The Reformation sponsored an expansion of Christian music through the writing of hymns and the composition of glorious music based on those hymns and the Gospels (see Bach, *The Passions of Matthew and John*). Yet the emphasis on austerity and simplicity in worship (see particularly the Puritans) inadvertently encouraged the development of drama on a secular basis (see Shakespeare's non-biblical world).

The Enlightenment in Europe began a process of secularization of Western culture that continues today.

The Enlightenment in Europe began a process of secularization of Western culture that continues today. Philosophy is completely removed from Christian premises and is often explicitly hostile to them (see Nietzsche). Art and music make use of Christian themes primarily through critique or parody (see Dali and Maplethorpe and Bernstein's *Mass*). Architecture expresses, not the communitarian ideal of Christianity, but the competitive aspirations of capitalism. As with its political dethronement, Christianity's cultural marginalization has stimulated conflicting responses among contemporary Christians. ∎

Essential Reading

H. R. Niebuhr, *Christ and Culture* (New York: Harper and Row, 1951).

Supplemental Reading

P. Murray, *The Oxford Companion to Christian Art and Architecture* (New York: Oxford University Press, 1996).

J. Pelikan, *Jesus through the Centuries: His Place in the History of Culture* (New York: Perennial Library, 1987).

L. Sweeney, *Christian Philosophy: Greek, Medieval, Contemporary Reflections* (New York: Peter Lang, 1997).

1. How does the history of art and architecture reflect the stages of Christianity's religious development and change?

2. What manifestations of Christianity illustrate the cultural stance of "Christ against the world"?

Christianity and Culture
Lecture 11—Transcript

In this penultimate lecture, we again consider Christianity in the world under the topic of religion and culture. In its long history, Christianity has engaged a range of cultures.

First was the Jewish symbolic world of Torah, shared by Jesus and the Apostles; then, the Greco-Roman culture of the Diaspora as Christianity moved into the ancient Roman Empire; and then, successively, the European, American, African, and Asian cultures.

Christianity has certainly been shaped by each of these cultural engagements, but Christianity has also helped shape culture. Even Judaism and Islam look differently because of the experience of Christianity.

It is, nevertheless, another of Christianity's paradoxes that a religion whose origins were so counter-cultural should find itself so entwined with culture over the course of its history. At the explicit level, the New Testament gives scant encouragement to a positive engagement with culture. Remember that the earliest expectation was that Jesus would be returning to judge the living and the dead within a very short period of time. Paul says in I Corinthians, chapter 7, that "the time is short and the frame of this world is passing away." That's scarcely an attitude that encourages one to get deeply involved in the forms of culture.

Indeed, the mysterious revelation through Jesus Christ is pitted explicitly against the wisdom of this world. In the Gospel of Luke, Jesus himself is quoted as saying, "I thank you, Father, Lord of heaven and earth, because you have hidden these things from the wise and the intelligent, and have revealed them to infants. Yes, Father, for such was your gracious will. All things have been handed over to me by my Father, and no one knows who the Son is except the Father, or who the Father is except the Son, and anyone to whom the Son chooses to reveal him."

Thus, in the words of Jesus, this deep wisdom is hidden from those who are wise in worldly ways, and is given to infants. In his first letter to the Corinthians, Paul likewise says that the wise in their wisdom did not know God, and so God had to reveal how true wisdom is to be found through the foolishness and the powerlessness of the cross of Christ.

In addition to this, the New Testament continues what some scholars call the "aconic tradition" of Israel. That is the tradition in Israel that God is not to be portrayed by any sort of image, and the New Testament has little attention given to beauty, to pleasure, or to human artistry. It is, among all the world's religious literature, perhaps the most lacking in any visual appreciation, or any sense of human *eros*, of human desire, and human love.

Yet there are indications already in the New Testament that Christianity was engaging culture. The letters of Paul and the letter to the Hebrews make good use of Greek rhetoric. They make arguments in the form of the rhetoric described by Aristotle, and we find elements of Greco-Roman popular moral philosophy in the writings of the New Testament.

The New Testament writers pick up the themes of friendship, envy, harmony, and contentment. It must also be acknowledged that the Christian belief in the incarnation that God has revealed through the human body of Jesus provides a basis for art. Clearly, if the body is worthwhile, then at some point Christianity is going to come to grips with pictorial representations of the body.

Finally, the stories of the Old Testament provide a rich cultural resource. There are the stories of Adam and Eve, of Cain and Abel, of Jacob and Esau, of David and Jonathan, and of Jonah and the great fish. The Old Testament is replete with the kinds of vivid stories and narratives that are lacking in the New Testament, and yet are taken over by Christians as part of their Scripture. These provide a rich resource for cultural exploitation.

Already in the second century, we find Christian apologists, those who are writing in defense of the Christian religion, confidently appropriating Platonic philosophy in a very explicit fashion. Justin Martyr, for example, follows a sort of standard philosophical commonplace when he talks about himself as investigated of several philosophical schools, trying each one and finding it inadequate until he came to Platonism, which he found the best of philosophies. Then he found Christianity, which was an even better philosophy.

From the start, Platonism was the form of Greek philosophy that Christians found most amenable. Plato's dialogs offer several very important perspectives that Christians found very conformable to their own beliefs.

Firstly, Plato placed revelation as superior to reason. In his argument with Protagoras, Plato argues that it is not humans who are the measure of all things, but God is the measure of all things. Plato also has a very strong admiration for *enthusiasmos*, for that possession of the spirit that comes upon poets and prophets.

Secondly, Plato's understanding of *eros* is not simply of a sexual desire, but rather a desire of the human spirit for the divine; *eros* is one that leads us to the divine. This is taken over particularly by St. Augustine, in his *Confessions* as an understanding of how the human spirit longs for God. As he says in the very first paragraph of his *Confessions*, "You have created us for yourself, oh God, and our hearts are restless until they rest in you." This was a very platonic understanding of rightly ordered *eros*.

Thirdly, in Platonism, the spirit is superior to the body, and again this fits beautifully with Christianity.

Finally, Platonism even offers a Demiurge who is at work in the creation of the world. This fits splendidly with the Christian understanding of the Christ as already preexistent and involved in the creation of the world in the beginning.

Platonism becomes the favorite Christian philosophy in its earliest centuries, and Christians even began to portray themselves in terms of a philosophical school. By the third century, Origen of Alexandria is able to enter into a very lengthy and complex argument with the neo-Platonic philosopher Celsus on pretty equal terms. Celsus had written a rebuttal of Christianity called the *True Discourse*, and in his work against Celsus, Origen enters into a long philosophically involved debate in defense of Christianity, fully confident that Christianity was the equal of neo-Platonism at the philosophical level.

Also, by the end of the second century and the beginning of the third century, we find the development of Christian art among wealthier Christians, especially funerary art in the decoration of tombs and in the decoration of sarcophagi. Therefore, we have an interweaving of biblical and pagan themes, so that sometimes it's difficult to figure out whether it's Pan who's being portrayed or the "Good Shepherd." Sometimes it's difficult to know whether what is being portrayed is the pagan rendition of soul *evictus,* the inconquerable son, or the Resurrection of Jesus.

Some themes are very clear. John the Baptist appears, Jesus sharing a meal with his disciples appears, and yes, Jonah and the great fish as a symbol of the Resurrection are portrayed already in the beginning of the third century as forms of distinctively Christian art.

Of course, the very earliest representation we have is the figure of the cross, scratched on the wall of a catacomb; in connection with the cross, we have that distinctive slogan, *Icthus Jesus Christos Theou Uios Soter,* or "Jesus Christ, Son of God." *Soter* is an acronym that spells "fish;" therefore, the symbol of the fish is a very early pictorial symbol for Christianity.

Also in the second century, we find the development of literature, the Apocryphal Gospels and the Apocryphal Acts that find as their closest analogy the picaresque novels, the romantic novels of the Greco-Roman world, like Leucippe and Clitophon.

Indeed, the closest analogy to the Acts of Paul and Thecla written around the year 1 A.D. is *Chaereas and Callirhoe*, a romantic novel. Boy meets girl, boy loses girl, boy finds girl. That was written by Chariton of Aphrodisias.

When Christianity becomes the imperial religion under Constantine, it obviously is going to appropriate even more explicitly many aspects of

Greco-Roman culture, even as it explicitly rejects paganism. It destroys the statues of the gods and appropriates the pagan temples and Christianizes them.

In the realm of thought, the development of Christian doctrine owed a great deal to its reliance upon philosophy. The doctrinal disputes of the fourth and fifth centuries were fundamentally ontological or philosophical in character. It was because the Alexandrian priest Arius tried to understand the Trinity in philosophical terms that he concluded that if God is one, the Son could not also be God; that is, if the Father is God, then the Son could not also be God, but had to be a creature. He therefore took the philosophical phrase *homoiousios*, meaning, "the son is only similar in nature to the father."

The Council of Nicea used similar philosophical language in the development of the Nicene Creed so as to rebut Arius by declaring that the Son is *homoousios*, the very "same substance as the Father." Philosophical language and the use of rational discourse in order to give propositional expression to the Christian experience was a manifestation of cultural development.

Under the Empire, Christian writers wrote poetry and hymns in honor of Christ that made use of classical forms. Gregory of Nazianzen, for example, wrote reams of theological poetry in the form of classical hexameters in Greek. In the West, Ambrose of Milan composed poetry in Latin that was chanted by members of the Christian community, in order to give hymnic expression to proper doctrine over against the Arian opponents. We even find in Greek literature, the equivalent of the invocation of the muses. Remember that the Homeric epics and Virgil begin their epics by invoking the muses to guide them in their discourse.

We find in Greek literature and in Christian literature that the equivalent of the invocation of the muses is a citation from a letter of James 1:17: "Every good and perfect gift comes down from above, from the Father of lights, with whom there is not change or shadow of alteration." They thereby signify that what they are writing is really a gift from God.

We saw in an earlier presentation that as the hierarchy of the church under Constantine paralleled the complex administration of the Empire, so did the occupation of great public spaces; the imperial basilicas encouraged the development of art. We saw how public worship in these basilicas became a great liturgy with dramatic movement and costumes or vestments, processions, song, smoke, and bells. All of this was highly dramatic, because it served as a kind of public spectacle.

At the same time, from the fourth century on, in basilicas like that at Ravenna, which is extant and a spectacular site, we have the adornment now by means of mosaics. The mosaics at Ravenna put in the *apse* of the basilica in the Great Arch, representations of the divine and of the political rulers as a kind of cooperative picture of the ruling of the world through Christian and imperial power.

Instead of statues of gods, we find the development of statues of saints in the same sort of fashion. I mentioned icons in an earlier presentation, especially with regard to the Orthodox tradition. The use of these icons, these pictorial images of Jesus, of Mary, of the saints, both private and public, was a perfect artistic representation of belief in the incarnation and in the sanctification, indeed, for the Orthodox, the divinization of humanity. As I pointed out earlier, they did not think of the production of icons as an artistic enterprise. It really was a spiritual exercise, and the representation was not meant to be appreciated aesthetically. It was meant to be a means of meditation and of contemplation of the mysteries of religion. If one enters, even today, an Orthodox church, however, one sees that the icons form the dividing point between the place of the laity and the place of the clergy, the sanctuary, in what is called an *iconostasis*. That is, the standing wall of icons in which all of the various pictorial representations are arranged, as symbols of how that sanctification actually occurs in humans as they move in and out of that sacred space.

In medieval Europe, the term "Christendom," as I mentioned earlier, expresses the complete integration of Christian religion and culture. Just as the Pope is supreme over the King on the political realm, at least in theory, so also in the world of learning, theology is regarded as the "Queen of the Sciences." Already in the 11th century, some of Canterbury had defined Christian theology as *"fides quaerens intellectus,"* "faith seeking understanding."

In the great medieval universities that sprang up in the 11th and 12th centuries in Bologna, in Oxford, and in Paris, Scholastic theology achieved a remarkable rapprochement between the Gospel and Christian theology shaped by Plato, but with a very powerful contribution made by Aristotle. Remember that Aristotle had been rediscovered and translated by Islamic scholars, and it was because of the Islamic philosophers Averroes and Avicenna, that Aristotle became available to Jewish philosophers, theologians like Maimonides, to Christian theologians like Thomas Aquinas, and played a big role in the shaping of what is called scholastic theology, as in the monument of learning called the *Summa Theologica* by Thomas Aquinas. Here, we find a combination of the spirit of transformation that is attributed to grace and the work of the Holy Spirit, brought into close connection with the virtue ethics of Aristotle.

We find also the influence of Aristotelian metaphysics. There is such confidence in being able to talk about the world, that Thomas Aquinas even offers the famous five rational proofs for the existence of God. Clearly, Aquinas did not think that one could simply make those proofs if one did not already believe in God, but nevertheless there was a great confidence in the marriage between reason and religion. Christian theology was, above all, a reasonable approach to God.

Similarly, in the great medieval cathedrals, cathedral comes from the word *cathedra*, which means the "bishop's seat," so the cathedral would be in the central church of a diocese. In the great cathedrals that spread across Europe, we find, in architecture, exhibits for the Christian story, in carvings and in stained glass. Even in the use of the Gospel book, we find the outlet for Christian art. Remember, before the invention of printing, all books were copied by hand; therefore, they were manuscripts, and in such magnificent examples as the *Book of Kells*, adorned by Celtic monks, we find exquisite artistic representations in the careful calligraphy and in the adornment of the initial letters that begin books and paragraphs.

Similarly, the stained glass windows of the cathedrals were famously called the *People's Bible*, because they represented the various Gospel stories in vivid pictorial fashion. I remind you of the power that such pictorial representations have. If any of you have seen the movie *Amistad*, you'll remember there is that marvelous scene in which the African slaves cannot read, but they see the pictures of the story of Jesus that is found in an illustrated Bible, and they figure out what the story means, and are deeply moved by the story simply because of these pictures.

Carvings within the church and outside the church, especially over the portal of the cathedral, frequently represented the communion of saints, all of the various Christians who had accomplished that goal of Christianity, which was personal transformation.

Finally, the liturgy of the Eucharist was in effect the cultural form of drama. It had become this spectacular performance that was put on by the clergy in costume, in vestments and so forth, in a foreign language, increasingly Latin, and was observed by the rest of the people. As I mentioned in an earlier presentation, the high point of the Eucharist in the Medieval period was not the consumption of the bread and the wine—the eating, as at a meal—but rather the showing of the host as a representation of transubstantiation—that through the almost magical words of the priest, ordinary bread and wine were truly changed into the body and blood of Christ. This was one reason why ordinary Christians grew more and more fearful of actually sharing in that meal, because they felt unworthy of taking on such a great honor.

Historians of drama also credit the scene of the Gospel at the empty tomb, when the women come to seek the body of Jesus, as a very early development of dramatic form. It's called the *Quem Quaeriti;* "Whom do you seek?" the angel asks, and the women respond. That dialogical form begins to construct the form of drama.

Finally, art was in music. There was the development of Gregorian chant, which was sung a cappella without any instrumental accompaniment, both at the mass or the Eucharist, and in the Divine Office, that is in the periods of prayer in which monks sang the Psalms every day, as a form of worship to God.

We find the development of music on the one side, very beautiful music, but on the other side of scriptural interpretation—because these musical settings also offered genuine interpretation of the words of Scripture, much as opera does with the libretto, and indeed many parts of the Eucharist—the antiphons, the canticles, and so forth, represent very intricate readings and understandings of Scripture.

The Renaissance and the Reformation, each in its fashion, developed and diminished the Christian form of culture. The culture of the Renaissance is, on the surface, still recognizably, indeed emphatically Christian, but at a deeper level it represents the recovery of Greco-Roman and pagan influence.

In music, painting, and sculpture, Christian themes abound. The polyphonic music of Palestrina is set to Christian themes. The frescos and sculpture of Michelangelo are obviously mostly scriptural.

Most famously, there is "The Last Supper" by Leonardo da Vinci, but what has changed? What has changed is that art serves the vanity of princes and of popes, especially the Renaissance popes, the Borges. The ideal of the body is more Greek than Christian, as we can see in Michelangelo's magnificent statue of David, or in the ceiling of the Sistine Chapel.

The rebirth of Platonic philosophy challenges the unified worldview of Scholasticism. When Greek is rediscovered, renaissance humanists, like Erasmus of Rotterdam, have to walk a very fine line between learning and Christianity, because the rediscovery of Greek is the rediscovery of Plato, and the rediscovery of Plato is to recognize the superiority both in thought and in aesthetics of Plato to Aristotle. Therefore, that medieval synthesis, which was the Gospel in Aristotle, is called into question.

Perhaps most dramatically, remember the previous lecture on politics, the "Donation of Constantine" on which the popes had rested all of their claims to political and material authority over Europe. Lorenzo Valla, on the basis of the analysis of language and of handwriting, demonstrated it to be a forgery. This was the beginning of critical scholarship and of a sense of critical historiography. All of these things had a very deep impact even though the influence of Christian themes continued.

In a similar fashion, the Reformation rejected the extravagance of medieval Catholicism in favor of a simpler and more scriptural Christianity. The reformers returned to an iconic approach to the visual arts. Notice that in Protestant churches, even today, there is a cross rather than a Crucifix. There is no bodily representation. But there still continue the marvelous carvings and etchings and paintings of artists like Albrecht Durer and his marvelous representations of the Book of Revelation.

The Reformation also influenced an expansion of Christian music. The Reformation found artistic expression mainly through music, through the writing of hymns by Martin Luther, the Wesleys, and the composition of glorious music based on the hymns and the gospels, leaving us such glorious monuments as Johann Sebastian Bach's *The Passions of Matthew and John.*

Yet the emphasis on austerity and simplicity in worship, especially among the Puritans, inadvertently encouraged the development of drama on a purely secular basis. Notice that Shakespeare's dramas have absolutely no influence from Scripture. Shakespeare lives in a completely non-biblical world, which is why Harold Bloom ascribes to Shakespeare the invention of the human. With the Enlightenment in Europe, we begin a process of secularization of Western culture that continues today. In philosophy, we find no trace of Christian premises, and the philosophy of people like Friedrich Nietzsche and Feuerbach are explicitly hostile to Christian premises. Art and music make use of Christian themes primarily through critique or parody: *The Last Supper* of Salvatore Dali, the photographs of Maplethorpe, Bernstein's *Mass.*

Architecture expresses not the communitarian ideal of Christianity, but the competitive aspirations of capitalism—not the cathedral or the basilica, but the skyscraper. As with its political dethronement, Christianity's cultural marginalization has stimulated conflicting responses among contemporary Christians. Some Christians today, especially evangelical Christians, want to create a separate but equal Christian culture: Christian rock and roll, Christian art themes, and Christian fiction.

Liberal Christians, in contrast, are eager to provide a cultural critique from the perspective of Christian values, but offer little specific Christian content to that critique. Christianity, as a religion, has lost both its political centrality, and—to a large extent—its cultural impact.

Tensions and Possibilities
Lecture 12

The future of Christianity may not lie in this First World. The future of Christianity may lie in what we now call the "Third World," or the developing nations.

Christianity has a long and complex story that is not yet over. Indeed, it may be entering into its fourth and most critical phase of development as a truly world religion. The first stage, of approximately 250 years, was that of birth and development, when Christianity was truly an intentional religious community forced to negotiate its identity in a pluralistic world without the support of culture or the state. The second stage was the long period (some 13 centuries) when Christianity was an established religion and the main form of culture in the West. The third stage, of about 2 centuries, consists in the struggle caused by cultural marginalization and political disestablishment. At the start of the 21st century, the Christian story is far from over. Indeed, Christians find themselves at a dramatic turning point of self-definition as they seek to discover which of the stages of its story best prepares it for the future.

In the First-World countries most shaped by the cultural forces of modernity, Christians are in some ways deeply divided and in some ways more united than at any time since the Reformation. Division is due less to disagreements on major points of doctrine concerning God or Christ, or even major moral stances, than to profoundly different stances toward modernity itself, especially on such issues as the authority of Scripture. The active-resistant response seeks to oppose modernity in the name of a distinctively Christian culture. Roman Catholicism and Evangelical Protestantism represent this stance. The passive-resistant stance refuses to acknowledge modernity and cultivates continuity with the past. This is the style of the Orthodox churches. The passive-accommodating stance seeks a positive engagement with modernity while maintaining loyalty to the heart of the Christian ethos. Mainline Protestant denominations tend to follow this path. The active-accommodating response is found in some liberal Protestant groups. Here, modernity sets the standard and Christianity seeks to conform itself to the dominant culture. Reading the Scriptures is something of a salvage operation—trying to determine which parts of the Scriptures should be dropped and which parts should still be considered. This approach has, paradoxically, been identified with certain Anglican bishops, with the Jesus Seminar, and much historical research on Jesus. Here, Christianity has to reinvent itself on the basis of the empirically revived Jesus.

Christians also made significant steps toward bridging traditional hostilities during the 20th century, moving from active rivalry toward fraternal acceptance in an ecumenical movement. Protestant denominations began cooperative social ventures and explored shared dimensions of faith and morality through the World Council of Churches. Conversation and cooperation replaced competition. Roman Catholicism joined the ecumenical movement through the Second Vatican Council (1963–1965), and Orthodoxy has also joined the conversation. The ideal of unity is sought less through a structural uniformity than through the recognition of a legitimate diversity in Christian life.

The future for Christianity, however, may lie less in the First World than in developing nations. The greatest numerical growth of Christianity has been found in Asia, Africa, and Latin America, as well as in the countries of Eastern Europe, where communism had forbidden religious practice; new Christians there are fervent. Correspondingly, Christians in Western Europe and North America decline in numbers and in enthusiasm. More pertinent for the future, Christianity outside of Europe and North America is creative, shedding the vestiges of colonialism and developing indigenous forms of Christian expression in liturgy and spirituality.

As it enters the fourth stage of its story, Christianity must decide how to move into the future, even as it recognizes that the decision is not entirely its own. Considered from the outside as a human institution, Christianity faces the challenge of deciding which aspects of its tradition are essential and which are optional. Considered from the inside as a believing community, Christianity must discern how God is at work in the world and shape its response accordingly. The future of this world religion appears to lie in its capacity to become a world religion. ■

Supplemental Reading

J. L. Fredericks, *Faith among Faiths: Christian Theology and Non-Christian Religions* (New York: Paulist Press, 1999).

M. Kinnamon and B. E. Cope, *The Ecumenical Movement: An Anthology of Key Texts and Voices* (Grand Rapids: Eerdmans, 1997).

H. Kung and H. Moltmann, eds., *Christianity and World Religions* (Concilium; Edinburgh: T & T Clark, 1986).

G. Marsden, *Fundamentalism and American Culture: The Shaping of Twentieth-Century Evangelicalism, 1870–1925* (New York: Oxford University Press, 1980).

Questions to Consider

1. What do the recent tendencies toward unification and the tendencies toward separation reveal about the contemporary challenge to Christianity as a world religion?

2. In light of its history to this point, how realistic is it to speak of Christianity as entering, not the end of its story, but a new and positive stage in its story?

Tensions and Possibilities
Lecture 12—Transcript

Twelve thirty-minute lectures are not much when dealing with any significant subject. When dealing with a world religion of the size, antiquity, and complexity of Christianity, 12 thirty-minute lectures seems really inadequate.

My treatment of Christianity has had to be very broad, and even though I've been sketching with a broad brush, I've had to leave out of the account any number of important subjects. We have not considered at all, for example, the experience of Christianity. What does it mean to experience what Christians claim they experience?

Nor have we been able to talk about that extraordinarily rich and broad intellectual tradition called Christian theology. I hope, however, that I've provided at least something of a roadmap to this world religion, a sense of where you might go to find out more of what interests you.

Since the course does come to an end, we must turn, in this final presentation, to some sort of consideration of Christianity in the beginning of the 21st century, both in its positive and in its negative aspects. Here, above all, I must warn you, it is one scholar's opinion, so let the auditor beware.

Christianity has had a long and complex story, as we have seen, but it is a story that is not yet over. Indeed, Christianity may be entering into its fourth and most critical phase of development as a truly "world" religion.

The first stage, of almost 250 years, extends from the death and Resurrection of Jesus, to the establishment of Christianity as the imperial religion under Constantine in the beginning of the fourth century. This was the period of birth and development, when Christianity truly was a persecuted minority, and an intentional community. That is, people belonged to it because they chose to belong to it, more than they were born into it, and it had to find its way within Jewish and Greco-Roman culture without the support of politics or of culture.

The second stage of Christianity was a long period, some 13 centuries after Constantine, when Christianity was an established religion and the main form of culture, or at least the main formative influence on culture both in the East and in the West. Much of our attention has been focused upon those two periods of Christianity.

The third stage of Christianity has lasted for roughly the last two centuries, and it has consisted of the struggle within and without Christianity; Christianity must now try to navigate through the world it now inhabits, one that has resulted from its cultural marginalization. This has occurred because of the *Enlightenment*, and because of its political disestablishment.

Two lectures ago, I talked about the political disestablishment that came about as a result of the American Revolution, the French Revolution, and the Russian Revolution. Christianity, in virtually every part of the world today, finds itself not as an established religion of the state, but rather as one religion among many, with no visible or explicit political support. I want to talk a little bit more about the cultural marginalization that I touched on in the last lecture, which really came about because of the Enlightenment in Europe, and I want to remind you of what we mean by the Enlightenment.

Of course, the term "Enlightenment" is sometimes resented by Christians because it implies that in fact people were really enlightened; that's a debatable point, but clearly the Enlightenment meant—at the very least—the assertion of human reason as the measure of all things, including revelation. This is a complete turnabout from antiquity. Remember that for Plato, as I mentioned in the last lecture, God was the measure of all things, not humans, and that's clearly the view shared by Christianity. As Anselm says, "Theology is faith seeking understanding." You begin with faith, and then human intelligence tries to figure out what that means.

The Enlightenment turned that around. Now, revelation has to answer at the court of human reason, and human reason itself is defined in a fairly narrow fashion. Not all ways of reasoning are considered to be equally valid. Rather, it's that form of reasoning, which can be empirically verified, that is the judge of all things. If we're in the realm of natural science, that is that which can be demonstrated through experimentation, replication, prediction, calculation, and so forth. If we're talking about history, it's that which can be empirically verified by means of evidence and so forth.

What happened within the Enlightenment is that Christianity had virtually every aspect of it challenged, including the whole claim to the supernatural. Its story was now challenged on grounds of its historicity. There develops in the 16th century in England, and then very quickly also in Germany, a form of Christianity called *deism*. It still bears the name "Christian," but in effect it has been reduced to what might be called "reasonable" in Christianity. A deist, like Thomas Jefferson in the United States, is somebody who cuts out of the Gospel everything involving miracles, the supernatural, and the sacraments, all of these kinds of things. Jesus is admired as a kind of heroic moral exemplar and wise teacher, but surely not as the powerful and risen Lord, which was proclaimed by traditional Christianity.

With the Enlightenment came the birth of modernity, the modern age, together with the political upheavals of revolution. This made the last 200 years of Christianity greatly confusing. We find, then, at the beginning of the 21st century, that the Christian story is far from over, despite the many obituaries that are written for Christians by its cultured despisers. Much to the chagrin of some of those cultured despisers, Christianity is booming; it is growing everywhere in the world. As we said in the very opening, over two billion of the world's population call themselves Christians.

Nevertheless, even though this story is not over, and Christianity is not going to die out, it is a critical stage in the story, because Christians are at a dramatic turning point of self-definition as they seek to discover what parts of their previous story best prepares them for the future. The question for Christianity, then, is: How will it look in its next stage?

What I want to do then in this lecture is to provide some kind of assessment of the state of Christianity in two large topics. I want to talk first about Christianity in the First-World nations, primarily Europe and the United States, or North America generally. These are the countries that are most shaped by the forces of modernity; the culture is most shaped by the

Enlightenment. Christians in Europe and in North America are, in some ways, more deeply divided than others. That's going to be my first topic. In other ways, Christians are more unified than they have ever been, but on two different sorts of planes.

Let me begin with the way in which they are more divided. Christians in First-World countries today are divided less because of major disagreements on points of doctrine, although even there, there are some disputes. Theology generally does not matter as much to people as it once did, though, so you rarely find an explicit debate, for example, over the divinity of Jesus among Christians. Most will ascribe at least verbally to the statements of the Creed. Nor are they divided primarily over moral issues, although issues such as abortion have certainly galvanized a great deal of disagreement among Christian communities; by and large, however, Christians agree on their moral stances.

The disagreements among Christians in the First World have much more to do with how Christianity should position itself over against modernity, especially with regard to the authority of Scripture, the future destiny of the world, and of Christians themselves. I want to provide something of a typology of four responses that we find among Christians today.

The first response might be called an active-resistant response. This is found largely today among evangelical Christians, sometimes called Fundamentalist Christians, and until 1964, among Roman Catholic Christians, primarily.

The active-resistant response seeks to oppose modernity, to simply reject the Enlightenment and all its ways, and indeed reject the political overturning of Christianity's power. It seeks to align itself with a distinctively Christian culture, if you will, to turn back the clock. Such Christians, earlier Roman Catholics, evangelical Christians, seek to create a separate but equal Christian culture that is unmarked by the values of modernity or of the Enlightenment. As I mentioned in the earlier lecture, Christian rock and roll, Christian education, and Christian art each represent separate values that reject the cultural values of modernity. Such Christians engage in polemics, they attack modernity, attack the ways of the Enlightenment, and they engage in apologetics. They write elaborate defenses of Christianity's view of the world and its posture.

With regard to Scripture, such Christians have tended to be fundamentalists in their approach. They take Scripture at its literal meaning and regard it as inerrant. They take the position that Scripture must be swallowed whole, if you will, without exercising the criticism of human reason. This sometimes becomes almost a marginal line of loyalty to the Christian tradition.

Paradoxically, the active-resistant response is, in some sense, most defined by modernity, because in fact by actively resisting, it actually accepts the categories of modernity as the categories that need to be fought. If the Enlightenment says that Scripture can only be true if it is literally true and historically true, the fundamentalist responds by saying, "Well, it is literally true and historically true if one accepts the very limited understanding of rationality that is offered by the Enlightenment," rather than saying, "My goodness, language can be true in a number of ways; it can be true mythically, it can be true poetically, or it can be true through metaphor, and so forth."

Thus, even though the active-resistant response is militantly opposed to modernity, it's also very much defined by modernity. It's impossible to think of contemporary evangelical Christians, let us say, in the 15th century. It simply would be unthinkable apart from the conditions of modernity.

A second response is what I call passive-resistant, and as the term suggests, this is the simple refusal to acknowledge modernity. This is found, as I suggested earlier, among the Orthodox traditions such as the Greek Orthodox and Russian Orthodox traditions; these have deliberately cultivated *hagia paradosis*, "holy tradition," continuity with the past. "Nothing has changed, therefore nothing needs to be addressed; we simply ignore modernity."

In terms of Scripture then, in terms of the way that the Bible is read, Orthodox theologians and preachers continue to read the Bible in Greek or in Russian in exactly the same way that the patristic authors of the fourth and fifth centuries read it. Indeed, their major authorities for what the Bible means are found in those ancient Greek writers. There is, in other words, no critical engagement with Scripture, but rather a total acceptance of revelation as dominant, without paying any attention at all to the six days a week when they are living in the modern world.

The third response, I call the passive-accommodating stance. This is characteristic of most mainline Protestant traditions in Europe and North America; after the second Vatican Council, from 1963 to 1965, it also became the stance of Roman Catholicism, especially in the United States.

The passive-accommodating stance seeks a positive engagement with modernity. That is, it accepts the fact that the Enlightenment has happened, that political revolution has overturned the establishment of Christianity, and that—in fact—Enlightenment is not bad. Tolerance is better than intolerance. Natural science is a good thing, historical enquiry is a good thing, and so it accepts modernity, but also wants to maintain loyalty to the heart of the Christian *ethos*. It wants to be truly Christian, but change, if you will, or adapt to the times.

The difficulty with this is that it's extraordinarily hard, after all of this long history, to figure out what the heart of the Christian *ethos* is, what parts of Christianity must faithfully be adhered to, and which parts of it we can let go in order to sort of be pertinent or relevant to the contemporary age.

In mainline Protestantism today, in Roman Catholicism today, in First-World countries, we find it's the use of the critical study of the Bible; scholars are educated, and they approach the Bible not as literally true and inerrant in every respect. It is true perhaps metaphorically, symbolically, religiously, but not necessarily historically, and they engage the text with critical intelligence, which is really the way that modernity engages text. Nevertheless, what distinguishes this group is a deep desire to be loyal to the religious message of Christianity, trying to hold onto the fundamentals while trying to negotiate the non-essentials.

The final posture is what I call the active-accommodating response, and this is found in Europe and North America among the most liberal Protestant groups, like Unitarians. This posture is sort of a continuation of the deist tradition that I talked about earlier. In this response, modernity sets the framework, and Christianity tries to find a place as best it can. This may sound a lot like the passive-accommodating stance, but it really is different.

In the passive-accommodating stance, there is the claim of equal loyalty to both and trying to negotiate it. In the active accommodation, it is assumed that modernity and modernity's understanding of reason and of the world is correct, and that Christianity has to find a place within that. You find, then, with regard to the reading of the Bible, for example, that this posture really emphasizes those parts of Scripture that are dangerous for people, those parts that are bad for women, those parts that are bad for people, that damage and injure people.

Reading Scripture in this way is something of a salvage operation, trying to find those bits that are still worth considering, even though a lot of it has to be jeopardized. This kind of approach has paradoxically been very much identified with certain Anglican bishops such as J.A.T. Robinson, in his infamous book *Honest To God*, which pretty much threw overboard a great deal of biblical revelation. More recently, the Bishop of Newark, John Spong, takes the position that the New Testament is fundamentally erroneous, and that Christianity has to redefine itself on the basis of historical investigation. This is the posture taken by the Jesus Seminar and by a lot of historical Jesus research.

Notice how the historical Jesus project is precisely the project of modernity. We want to recover and discover a "historical" Jesus, not the one revealed in Scripture. Christianity has to kind of reinvent itself on the basis of that empirically derived figure.

Christians, consequently, have these dramatic differences in their responses, and the hostilities between them tend to be at that level; who is critical and who is loyal? On one side, loyalty means you can't think critically. On the other side, if you're going to think critically, you have to be disloyal. To find kind of a middle position in which loyalty to the tradition and the use of critical intelligence are combined is a very difficult place to occupy.

I also said that Christians in the 20th century began to make significant steps toward bridging traditional hostilities, moving from active rivalry between denominations. I'm talking about denominations now: Catholic, Protestant, Orthodox, Baptist, Lutheran, and so forth. This change from active rivalry and hostility toward fraternal understanding is found in a movement called the ecumenical movement. The term "ecumenical" means "universal," and this is a movement in the 20th century toward Christian unity.

It must be said immediately that the ability of Christians to fight each other on the basis of the name of Christ, and in terms of politics and violence, has not disappeared completely. Northern Ireland is an outstanding example of this. The battles between Orthodox and Catholics in Croatia and Bosnia is another example.

Really, up until the 1960's, those who grew up in the United States were well aware of the intolerance between Christian groups. Catholics were not allowed to marry Protestants without special dispensations. When John F. Kennedy, as a Roman Catholic, was running for president, there was an outbreak of violent anti-Catholicism on the part of many Protestant groups.

Nevertheless, despite this sort of residue of those ancient European hostilities during the 20th century, in the 1920's, Protestant denominations began to seek a form of unity. They said, "We're just killing each other," and so they began to unify by joining in practical projects, helping people, and engaging in social welfare. Slowly, by working together, they began to gain an appreciation of each other, and in 1948 the World Council of Churches was created.

The World Council of Churches is a Protestant organization that seeks ecumenism, that is, unity among Christian bodies. The great resistor of this was Roman Catholicism, but in 1963 to 1965, the greatest event in Roman Catholicism in 500 years occurred. That was the Second Vatican Council. It was called by a very unlikely person, Pope John XXIII, who was an elderly man and thought to be something of a caretaker Pope. The Pope turned out to be a revolutionary, and he summoned a great council of Catholic bishops from around the world, in 1963, in order to accomplish what he called *adjournamento*. In Italian it means "getting up to date," becoming relevant, and for Pope John XXIII, Catholicism needed to reverse its recent history, rather than condemning modernity and the Enlightenment.

One might remember that Pope Pius X in the beginning of the 20th century condemned, as a heresy, Modernism, and condemned, as a heresy, interestingly enough, Americanism, specifically the notion that democracy was the best way to order a government as opposed to a monarchy. This was reversing the sort of totalitarian position of Roman Catholicism and its exclusiveness.

Consequently, this great council was called, and interestingly enough, Protestant observers, experts, and religious leaders were invited to the council, and came. This was the greatest gathering of Christian leaders of all denominations in centuries, in an amicable atmosphere.

In terms of internal Catholic life, the council is important because it really did turn Catholicism toward the modern world. Notice that under the influence of the American Jesuit, John Courtney Murray, the Roman Catholic Church came out in favor of religious freedom for the first time in its history, rather than in favor of the suppression of heresy. In addition, vis-a-vis Protestantism, the council issued decrees on other religions, and joined the ecumenical movement.

Since the 1960's, then, both Protestant and Catholic Christians have been joining in what is called "dialogue," a conversation about how they might emphasize what joins them rather than what separates them; recently, Orthodoxy has joined that conversation as well.

The ideal of unity can be pursued in one of two ways. The least likely way is to get everybody in the same organization, and although many church leaders have sweated many hours in trying to resolve the ancient disputes, for example, between Catholics and Lutherans over the doctrine of justification by faith or by works, nobody cares; those are the debates of the 16th century, not of the 21st century. It's unlikely that all Christians are going to belong to the same organization. Too many different cultures of Christianity have developed over time.

The other approach to ecumenism, which I think is much more attractive, is for Christians to recognize their diversity, and to celebrate it, to emphasize those elements that they share in terms of faith, morals, story, and so forth. They can learn from each other the many different styles in which one might live out an authentic Christian life. In other words, this is a shift from rivalry, envy, and hostility to one of mutual acceptance within the same framework of faith.

I want to say at the end, however, that the future of Christianity may not lie in this First World. The future of Christianity may lie in what we now call the "Third World," or the developing nations. The greatest numerical growth of Christianity over the last decade has been in Asia, Africa, and Latin America, as well as in those countries of Eastern Europe, including Russia, where communism for decades had forbidden religious practice.

New Christians in Eastern Europe are deeply fervent; notice that the current Roman Catholic Bishop of Rome, John Paul II, is Polish, has staunchly opposed communism, and has been a great celebrator of the development of the Christian tradition in Eastern Europe. Correspondingly, even as Christianity has grown numerically in Eastern Europe, Asia, Africa, and Latin America, it has tended to decline numerically, and in terms of enthusiasm, in North America and in Europe. I am willing to bet that the next Pope may well be from Asia or Africa, so numerous have the number of Asian and African cardinals, those who elect the Bishop, become.

More importantly for the future, Christianity outside of Europe and North America is creative. It has shed the vestiges of *colonialism*. You remember how the church in Latin America, Asia, and Africa had resulted from missions from Europe; these accompanied world exploration, and very much imported Western culture with Christianity.

What is happening now is that Christianity in those continents is becoming indigenous. It is discovering how to be Asian Christianity, African

Christianity, both in its liturgy and in its forms of spirituality. We now have very fine Indian Christian theologians, Latin American theologians, and Korean theologians. Indeed, many dioceses in the United States have become missionary. In other words, many Catholic parishes in this country are actually supplied with ministry by Vietnamese priests, by Colombian priests, and by Polish priests. The Third World may well be the future for Christianity.

As it enters the fourth stage of its story, Christianity needs to decide how to move into the future, even as it recognizes that that decision is not entirely its own to make. Considered from the outside as a human institution, Christianity faces the challenge of deciding which aspects of its tradition are essential, and which aspects of its tradition are optional. Considered from the inside as a believing community, Christians are challenged to discern how God is at work in the world, and to shape their responses accordingly. The future of this world religion, however, appears to lie in its capacity to truly become a world religion, rather than simply a remnant of a European culture that has run out of steam.

Timeline

c. 29–32 .... Ministry and Crucifixion of Jesus.

34–64/68 .... Paul's ministry and correspondence.

64 .... Persecution under Nero.

68–100 .... New Testament written.

70 .... Destruction of Temple in Jerusalem.

96 .... Persecution under Domitian.

115 .... Martyrdom of Ignatius of Antioch.

135–155 .... Marcion and Valentinus flourish.

150–215 .... Clement of Alexandria flourishes.

165 .... Martyrdom of apologist Justin.

160–225 .... Irenaeus and Tertullian flourish.

184–254 .... Life of Origen of Alexandria.

251–336 .... Antony of Egypt.

260–340 .... Life of the historian Eusebius of Ceasarea.

303 .... Great Persecution under Diocletian.

313 .... Constantine issues Edict of Milan.

325 .... Ecumenical Council at Nicea.

347–407...Life of John Chrysostom, great preacher and theologian in Orthodox tradition.

354–430...Life of Augustine of Hippo.

381...Council of Constantinople under Theodosius I; theological dominance of Cappadocians (Gregory, Basil, Gregory).

451...Council at Chalcedon: two natures in Christ.

c. 525..Benedict of Nursia founds monastery at Monte Cassino, writes *Rule for Monks.*

532–537...Great church of *Hagia Sophia* constructed in Constantinople.

590–604...Rule of powerful pope, Gregory I.

596...Mission to England.

673–735...Life of Venerable Bede, historian and interpreter of Scripture.

723...Mission to Germanic peoples.

726...Iconoclast controversy.

742–814...Charlemagne, "Holy Roman Emperor."

863–885...Cyril and Methodius, mission to Slavic peoples.

910...Monastery founded at Cluny, source of reform.

Timeline

1054	Schism between Eastern (Greek) and Western (Latin) church.
1095–1099	First crusade.
1100–1160	Peter Lombard, beginnings of Scholasticism.
1170–1221	Saint Dominic, founder of "Order of Preachers" (Dominicans).
1182–1226	Francis of Assisi, founder of mendicants.
1202–1204	Fourth crusade; sacking of Constantinople.
1225–1274	Thomas Aquinas, great Scholastic theologian.
1265–1321	Life of Dante, author of *Divine Comedy*.
1330–1384	John Wycliffe, English reformer and translator of the Bible.
1330–1400	English mystics flourish (Julian, Rolle, Hilton).
1340–1400	Geoffrey Chaucer, author of *Canterbury Tales*.
1370–1400	Czech reformer John Hus.
1453	Constantinople falls to Turkish Muslims; age of exploration begins.

1483–1546... Martin Luther, German reformer.

1484–1531... Ulrich Zwingli, Swiss reformer.

1489–1556... Thomas Cranmer, key figure in establishing the Church of England, leading author of *Book of Common Prayer* (1549).

1495–1498... Leonardo da Vinci paints *Last Supper.*

1504.. Michelangelo's *David* completed.

1509–1564... John Calvin, French reformer.

1513–1572... John Knox, Scottish reformer.

1517.. Luther's Ninety-five Theses.

1534.. Divorce of Henry VIII, beginning of the Church of England.

1540.. Jesuits founded by Ignatius of Loyola to defend faith and the pope.

1542–1621... Robert Bellarmine, Catholic reformer.

1545–1563... The Council of Trent.

1564–1616... Shakespeare.

1564–1642... Galileo.

1582.. Congregationalist churches in England.

1596–1650...................................... Rene Descartes, French philosopher who, with the British philosophers Locke and Hume, anticipate the Enlightenment and deism.

1612... Baptist churches in England.

1624–1691...................................... George Fox, founder of Quakers.

1685–1750...................................... Johann Sebastian Bach.

1694–1788...................................... Voltaire.

1703–1758...................................... American theologian Jonathan Edwards.

1703–1791...................................... John Wesley, with his brother Charles, founder of the Methodists in England and America.

1726–1750...................................... The Great Awaking in America.

1756–1791...................................... Wolfgang Amadeus Mozart.

1774... Shakers founded in America under Mother Ann Lee.

1776... American Declaration of Independence.

1782–1849...................................... William Miller and Adventist movement.

1788–1866...................................... Alexander Campbell, founder of Disciples of Christ.

1789... French Revolution.

1869–1870...................................... First Vatican Council (papal infallibility).

1948.. World Council of Churches founded in Amsterdam.

1962–1965...................................... Second Vatican Council.

Glossary/Biographical Notes

Apocrypha: From the Greek for "hidden things," the term refers to books not included in the canon of Scripture.

Apologist: One who makes a reasoned defense of the Christian faith, often in the face of attack; from the Greek, "make a defense."

Apostle: Literally, "one sent on a commission" to represent another as an agent. In early Christianity, leaders who were either chosen by Jesus or were witnesses of the Resurrection.

Asceticism: A way of life characterized by discipline and the avoidance of the pleasures of the body. In Christianity, often connected with a dualistic view of the world.

Augustine (354–430): Bishop of Hippo in North Africa and one of the most influential of Latin theologians.

Baptism: Literally a "dipping," the ritual of initiation already practiced by John the Baptist and everywhere attested among Christians from the start. It is universally recognized as a sacrament, though traditions differ as to timing (infant/adult) and the need to be "rebaptized in the spirit."

Barth, Karl (1886–1968): Important Protestant theologian whose "neo-Orthodoxy" provided a powerful antidote to liberal tendencies in Protestantism.

Benedict of Nursia (480–550): The writer of the *Rule for Monks* and the real founder of monasticism as it thrived in the West.

Bernard of Clairvaux (1090–1153): The abbot of the Benedictine monastery at Clairvaux and a powerful preacher and mystic.

Bishop: The Greek term *episcopos* means an "overseer" or "superintendent." In Roman Catholicism and Orthodoxy (and Anglo-Catholic versions of Protestantism), the head of a diocese who can ordain other ministers (priests).

Book of Common Prayer: The literary masterpiece of Thomas Cranmer, this is the official liturgical book of the Anglican (Episcopalian) tradition.

Byzantium: The name often given to the city of Constantinople (present-day Istanbul), the "New Rome" that Constantine founded; thus, the "Byzantine Empire."

Canon: The Greek term means "rule" or "measure." The official list of books included in the Christian Scripture, Old and New Testaments. The specific number of books included differs in Catholic and Protestant traditions.

Celibacy: The state of being unmarried. In Roman Catholicism, a requirement for male clergy at every level. In Orthodoxy, required of bishops but not of all priests.

Charismatic: Often used synonymously with *Pentecostal*, referring to the spiritual gifts that believers are given by the Holy Spirit, including the ability to prophesy and speak in tongues.

Christology: The understanding of the person and work of Jesus the Messiah = Christ. The differences in this doctrine caused major conflicts in Christianity in the 4th and 5th centuries.

Communion of Saints: The conviction that all the faithful, both the living and the dead, are joined in a fellowship, whether at the Eucharist or through other spiritual bonds.

Constantine (d. 337): The first Christian emperor, whose conversion and edict of toleration (the Edict of Milan in 313) reversed the political and cultural fortunes of Christianity.

Constantinople: The "New Rome" founded by Constantine and the religious and political rival of Rome from the 4th century forward.

Council of Trent: The Roman Catholic response to the Reformation in a series of reforming meetings between 1545–1563. Decisively shaped the Catholic church for the next 400 years.

Covenant: A binding agreement between two parties; in the Bible, between God and humans. Also, *Testament*. Christians understand Jesus to have initiated a "New Covenant," and the Christian writings form the "New Testament."

Cranmer, Thomas (1489–1556): Much more than Henry VIII, the guiding force of the reformation of the church in England. The main author of *The Book of Common Prayer*.

Creed: From the Latin *credo*, "I believe," a formal statement of belief. Christians recite either the Apostles' Creed or the Nicene Creed in their worship.

Crusades: Between the 11th and 13th centuries, a series of military expeditions sponsored by popes and Christian kings in an effort to wrest control of the Holy Land from the Muslims.

Deacon: From the Greek for "servant/minister," an order of ministry lower than that of the priest and characterized by service of helping, especially in liturgy.

Denomination: A specific church group that is united in its belief, morals, and most particularly, its polity and style of worship. Protestantism is made up of many denominations, such as Baptist, Methodist, and Presbyterian.

Diocese: The territory and population governed by a bishop in the traditions that have an episcopacy. An *archdiocese* is either a particularly important diocese or one that governs others; in the same fashion, *archbishop*.

Divine Office (also, *work of God*): The round of prayer through the day, based on the recitation of the Psalms, observed by monks.

Doctrine: Literally, a "teaching." In Christianity, the formal teaching on matters of faith is sometimes referred to as *dogma*.

Dualism: An explanation of the world in terms of equal and opposing principles. Marcion was dualistic, because he pitted evil matter against good spirit.

Easter: In the liturgical year, the celebration of the Resurrection of Jesus, three days after Good Friday, the day on which he was crucified.

Ecumenical Council: An official meeting of bishops from throughout the world. The first seven councils are generally regarded as ecumenical and authoritative. The Second Vatican Council was also an ecumenical council to which Protestants and Orthodox leaders sent "observers."

Ecumenism: The term used for the movement toward Christian unity in the 20th century; also *ecumenical movement*.

Edict of Milan: The declaration of tolerance enacted by Constantine in 313 that gave Christians freedom to practice their faith.

Elder: The same Greek term *presbyteros* is rendered as "priest" by Roman Catholics and "elder" by Protestants. In Protestant denominations, the elder is a leader who may or may not also minister sacramentally.

Enlightenment: The term used to designate the intellectual movement in the 17th and, especially, 18th centuries in Europe (and, to some extent, America) that elevated human reason to a position of superiority to revelation. One of the fundamental elements of "modernity."

Episcopal: The form of church governance in which authority flows from the top (the bishop) down to the people (laity), often through the agency of the clergy (priests).

Erasmus, Desiderius (1469–1536): The great Dutch humanist and translator of the New Testament who had a great influence on reformers, even though he remained faithful to Rome.

Eschatology: From the Greek for "last things," the understanding of what happens at the end of time or at the end of an individual's life. All Christians have an eschatology, but they differ greatly in their understandings of it.

Eucharist: The Greek term means "thanksgiving," and it was used in early Christianity for prayer, then became restricted to the sharing of the meal at which the death and resurrection of Jesus is commemorated; see also **Mass** and **Liturgy**. The sacrament of the Eucharist, together with baptism, is recognized by all Christians, though they differ in the significance of the symbolism.

Eusebius of Caesarea (260–340): The first real historian of Christianity and the enthusiastic biographer of Constantine the Great.

Faith: A complex term in Christianity. It includes "belief" but also means a commitment of the mind and heart to God and to Christ; therefore, "obedience of faith." Sometimes it refers to a "theological virtue" (together with hope and love), which is a disposition that is supposed to mark Christians in their lives.

Filioque: The Latin means "and the Son." It was added to the Nicene Creed by Carolingian theologians and caused considerable trouble with Eastern Christians; one of the factors leading to the great schism of the 11th century between East and West.

Franciscans: The order of mendicants begun by Francis of Assisi (1182–1226), who challenged the church to reform through the observance of evangelical poverty.

Gentiles: In ancient Mediterranean culture, all those who were not Jews. The Gentiles quickly became the dominant part of the Christian membership, and after the 2nd century, we hear practically nothing of Jewish Christians.

Glossolalia: The Greek term means "speaking in tongues," which Paul identifies as one of the gifts of the Holy Spirit and which charismatic or Pentecostal Christians see as a sign of being rebaptized by the Holy Spirit. Although some consider tongues real speech ("foreign languages"), it is a form of ecstatic babbling.

Gnosticism: The Gnostics were "in the know" (the Greek term suggests knowledge). A major, if diffuse, movement in the 2nd and 3rd centuries in Christianity, tending to expand the ideas of revelation and privilege to an individualistic understanding of the religion. Though opposed vigorously by Orthodox teachers, it has reappeared in various forms of "spiritual" Christianity, such as Albigensianism.

Gospel: The Greek word *euangelion* means "good news," and the first sense of this term is the basic message of what God accomplished in the death and resurrection of Jesus. Then, it came to mean the narrative accounts of Jesus's ministry, thus, "the Gospel of Mark."

Grace: The Greek word *charis* means "favor" or "gift," and Christians understand everything that has happened to them through Christ to be grace—something they do not deserve and can never earn.

Hellenism: In the broadest sense, the Greek culture of the time of earliest Christianity, which was taken over by the Roman Empire and was the context within which Christianity developed in its first five centuries.

Heresy: The Greek term *hairesis* means a "party" or "opinion." In Christianity, it has come to be understood as a misunderstanding or distorted understanding of doctrine. Thus, *heresy* is opposite *orthodoxy*, but it depends on who is talking!

Hermit: An individual who lives in solitude for the sake of complete devotion to prayer and worship. The form of monasticism begun by Antony in Egypt. In the Middle Ages, male and female hermits were sometimes called anchorites.

Holy Spirit: The power from God that was experienced through the Resurrection of Jesus and later defined as the "third person" of the Christian trinity.

Icon: From the Greek "image," a pictorial representation of God; the saints' devotion to icons plays a key role in Orthodox spirituality.

Iconoclasm: The term means the "breaking of images." In Orthodoxy, resistance to the iconoclastic movement between the 4th and 9th centuries was defining of the tradition, elevating the devotion of icons (images). Among Puritan Protestants also, images were regarded as idolatrous.

Iconostasis: In Orthodox churches, the screen, adorned with icons, that sets off the sanctuary from the rest of the church.

Ignatius of Antioch (d. 115): A bishop of the church in Antioch who, on his way to martyrdom, wrote seven letters to churches in Asia and Rome.

Incarnation: The doctrine that the second person of the trinity, the Son, became fully human, so that Jesus is both human and divine.

Inerrant: "Without error." A conviction that some Christians hold with regard to Scripture (Fundamentalists) and others, with regard to the church.

Infallible: Much like inerrant but used particularly in Roman Catholicism for papal authority in certain circumstances.

Inquisition: The ecclesial organization that was established in the 13th century for the prosecution of heresies (including Judaism); a symbol of intolerance and sometimes violence.

Inspiration: The conviction that God's Holy Spirit can find expression, that is "word," through human agents (the prophets) or writings (the Bible).

John the Baptist: According to the Gospel of Luke, the cousin of Jesus. According to the other Gospels (and the Jewish historian Josephus), a powerful preacher of repentance before Jesus.

Justification (also *righteousness*): The state or condition of being in right relationship with God.

Justin Martyr (d. 165): A Christian apologist who opposed the heretic Marcion and suffered martyrdom.

Liturgy: From the Greek for "public work," the official worship of the church, especially the Eucharist, or Lord's Supper, or Mass, but including as well the Divine Office.

Martyr: From the Greek word for "witness," someone who endures death for the sake of a conviction. In Christianity, one who dies because of witnessing to Christ.

Mary: The mother of Jesus. According to the Gospels, a virgin girl of Galilee who gave birth to Jesus through the power of the Holy Spirit. In both Orthodoxy and Roman Catholicism, the most revered figure next to Jesus himself: "Queen of the Saints."

Mass: The name traditionally used in Roman Catholicism (its derivation is uncertain) for the Eucharist, or Lord's Supper.

Mendicants (also *friars*): Members of the itinerant religious orders forbidden to have personal property, above all, the Franciscans and offshoots.

Messiah: In Hebrew, "the anointed one" and, in Greek, "Christ." The Jewish expectation for a figure to restore the people.

Millennialism (also *millenarian*): The expectation that God will visibly triumph in the future on earth in a thousand-year reign of the saints.

Mysticism: In every religion, the effort or process aimed at a direct experience of or union with the divine, especially through prayer and meditation.

New Testament: The 27 compositions in Greek that constitute the Christian portion of the Bible.

Nicene Creed: The statement of faith devised by the Orthodox bishops in response to Arius at the Council of Nicea in 325; later expanded by the Council of Constantinople in 381.

Old Testament: The compositions of the Hebrew Bible (read by the first Christians in the Greek translation called the Septuagint) to which the writings of the New Testament were appended to form the Christian Bible.

Origen (184–254): The greatest Scripture scholar and theologian of early Christianity, whose reputation was hurt by the excesses of some enthusiastic followers.

Original Sin: The conviction that the Fall by Adam and Eve fundamentally shaped the human experience until redemption through Christ.

Orthodoxy (see **Heresy**): The Greek term means "right teaching" or "right opinion." The opposite of heresy. Also applied to the Orthodox tradition in distinction to Roman Catholicism and Protestantism.

Paul the Apostle (d. 64 or 68): Originally a persecutor of the infant Christian movement, he became its most famous first-generation exponent, associated especially with the conversion of Gentiles and the writing of letters that became part of the New Testament. A highly controversial figure; see the Teaching Company course *Paul the Apostle*.

Penance: In general, "doing penance" means repenting of sins, or accepting the just punishment for sin. The term was used in Orthodoxy and Roman Catholicism for the sacrament that is now usually called the "Sacrament of Reconciliation."

Pentecost: The Jewish feast 50 days after Easter, which according to the Acts of the Apostles, was when the Holy Spirit came on Jesus's followers, "giving birth" to the church. An important feast of the liturgical year.

Pentecostal (also *charismatic*): A Christian for whom the visible manifestation of the gifts of the Holy Spirit—especially speaking in tongues—is the distinguishing mark of authentic Christianity.

Persecutions: The series of efforts—some local, some systemic—to eliminate the Christian movement through force. The first by the Roman state was under Nero in 64, and the greatest was under Diocletian in 303.

Peter (d. 64): The follower of Jesus who became, with Paul, an apostle and martyr. Two letters are attributed to him in the New Testament, and by legend, he was the first bishop of Rome.

Pilgrimage: The practice of traveling (often in groups) to a place considered holy to gain benefit from the power present through the influence of the saint or martyr commemorated at that location.

Pontius Pilate: Roman procurator in Judea under whom Jesus was executed.

Pope (also the *papacy*): From the 4th century on, this title was used for the Bishop of Rome.

Priest (see also **Elder**): Derived from the Greek *presbyteros*, a rank of ministry in the Orthodox, Roman Catholic, and Anglo-Catholic traditions, below that of the bishop. Can celebrate all the sacraments but not ordain other ministers.

Purgatory: In Roman Catholicism, a place of purgation in which, after death, the soul may be cleansed of venial sins in order to be fit to enter into the divine presence (heaven).

Reformation: The general name given to the efforts to reform the church in the 16th century. Usually used with reference to the Protestant Reformation (Luther, Calvin, and others) but can also be used of Roman Catholic efforts that are sometimes designated as the *Counter-Reformation* (as in the Council of Trent).

Relics: Literally, "remains"; usually the material remains of a martyr or saint that are venerated and thought to have power.

Renaissance: Literally, "rebirth"; the intellectual and cultural movements in Europe from the 14th to the 16th centuries that ended the medieval period and provided a transition to the modern era.

Resurrection: Rising from the dead; in the first place, that of Jesus and, in the second, the expectation for all those who die "in Christ" to share God's life.

Sacrament: In the broad sense, an outward sign that effects what it symbolizes. Christians recognize different numbers of rituals as sacraments, from two (baptism and Eucharist) to seven (baptism, Eucharist, confirmation, holy orders, marriage, reconciliation, anointing of the sick—or extreme unction).

Sanctification: Becoming holy; the process of transformation into the image of Christ. The goal of Christian existence is to become a "saint."

Sanctuary: In the Christian church, that part of the building that is regarded as particularly sacred, because of the presence of the Eucharist, the altar, or the pulpit or because it is the place where worship happens.

Scholasticism: The term used for the educational system of the medieval schools, especially for the methods of argumentation and debate found in the great universities, such as that of Paris. From the 11th century, Scholastic philosophy and theology forged a synthesis of Christianity and Greek philosophy (especially Aristotle).

Sin: In Christianity, more than an error or failure, a deliberate act of disobedience to God's will.

Synoptics: The collective term used for the Gospels of Matthew, Mark, and Luke. They are sufficiently similar to be arranged in three parallel columns (thus, "seen together") and, undoubtedly, are literarily interdependent. Most scholars think Mark was written first and was used by Matthew and Luke.

Torah: Jewish designation for the first five books of the Bible but also for the entire tradition of lore and learning derived from the Bible as a whole.

Trinity: The Christian understanding of God is that there is only one God— that is, the ultimate power who creates all from nothing—and that this one God exists in three persons, the Father, the Son, and the Holy Spirit. This understanding of the inner nature of God is derived from the specifically Christian experience of God in Jesus Christ (the Son) and through the Holy Spirit.

Uniat: The term used to refer to church bodies that are Orthodox in theology and ritual yet are in union with Rome.

Vatican: The section of Rome that is the residence of the pope and the central administration of the Roman Catholic church.

Bibliography

Essential Readings:

Writings from the New Testament can be read in any modern translation, such as the Revised Standard Edition; see *The New Oxford Annotated Bible: Revised Standard Edition*, edited by H. G. May and B. M. Metzger (New York: Oxford University Press, 1978). Guidance through the biblical literature is given by *The New Interpreter's Bible: A Commentary in Twelve Volumes*, edited by L. E. Keck (Nashville, TN: Abingdon Press, 1998). A sense of changing biblical interpretation is gained from *The Cambridge History of the Bible*, vol. 1: *From Beginnings to Jerome*, edited by P. R. Ackroyd and C. F. Evans (Cambridge University Press, 1970); vol. 2: *From the Fathers to the Reformation*, edited by G. W. H. Lampe (Cambridge University Press, 1969); and vol. 3: *The West from the Reformation to the Present Day*, edited by S. L. Greenslade (Cambridge University Press, 1963).

For other Christian literature in addition to the works listed separately, see *Ante-Nicene Fathers: The Writings of the Fathers down to A.D. 325* (8 volumes), edited by A. Roberts and J. Donaldson (reprint of 1885 edition; Peabody, MA: Hendrickson Publishers, 1994); *Nicene and Post-Nicene Fathers* (first series, 14 volumes), edited by P. Schaff (reprint of 1886 edition; Peabody, MA: Hendrickson Publishers, 1994); *Nicene and Post-Nicene Fathers* (second series, 14 volumes), edited by P. Schaff and H. Wace (reprint of 1890 edition; Peabody, MA: Hendrickson Publishers, 1994); and *The Classics of Western Spirituality* (104 volumes), edited by R. J. Payne et. al. (New York: Paulist Press, 1978–2002). For excerpts, see C. L. Manschreck (ed.), *A History of Christianity: Readings in the History of the Church from the Reformation to the Present* (Englewood Cliffs, NJ: Prentice-Hall, 1964).

The best single-volume reference work is the superb *Oxford Dictionary of the Christian Church*, edited by F. L. Cross, 3rd edition by E. A. Livingstone (New York: Oxford University Press, 1997). Other useful references include: J. D. Douglas (ed.), *The New International Dictionary of the Christian Church*, revised edition (Grand Rapids, MI: Zondervan Press, 1978); J. C.

Brauer, *The Westminster Dictionary of Church History* (Philadelphia, PA: Westminster Press, 1971); F. X. Weiser, *Handbook of Christian Feasts and Customs* (New York: Harcourt Brace Jovanovich, 1952); and *The New Catholic Encyclopedia*, 2nd edition, 14 volumes (New York: Thomson, Gale, 2002).

Students who wish to get a start can do no better than with the first Essential Reading listed for the first lecture, M. J. Weaver, *Introduction to Christianity*, 3rd edition, with D. Brakke and J. Bivins (Belmont, CA: Wadsworth, 1998).

Supplementary Readings:

Abbott, W. M., S.J. *The Documents of Vatican II*. New York: Guild Press, 1966. An English translation of the documents of the council that brought Roman Catholicism into conversation with the modern world, together with commentary by participants.

Ahlstrom, S. *A Religious History of the American People*. New Haven: Yale University Press, 1972. Highly readable (it won the 1973 National Book Award), this study by the dean of American religious historians is also comprehensive.

Anderson, W. K. *Protestantism: A Symposium*. Nashville, TN: Commission on Courses of Study, Methodist Church, 1944. This set of essays provides viewpoints on a variety of topics, from the early reformers, to basic Protestant principles, to church music.

Aumann, J. (with others). *Monasticism: A Historical Overview*. Still River, MA: St. Bede's Publications, 1984. A small but illuminating set of essays by monastic authors on the monastic tradition from its origins to the present day.

Bainton, R. H. *The Reformation of the Sixteenth Century*. Boston. Beacon Press, 1952. A classic treatment of the pivotal events and persons that decisively changed Christianity in Europe.

Bibliography

Benedict of Nursia, *The Rule of Saint Benedict.* Trans. By L. Doyle. This 6th-century composition drew from the best of the earlier movements to create a stable form of monasticism—combining "prayer and work" in the frame of a "school of the Lord's service"—that would prove widely influential.

Benz, E. *The Eastern Orthodox Church: Its Thought and Life*, translated by Richard and Clara Winston. Garden City, NJ: Doubleday, 1963. An introduction to the Orthodox tradition that pays particular attention to its distinctive theological tendencies.

Binding, G. *High Gothic: The Age of the Great Cathedrals*. London: Taschen, 1999. With color illustrations, a treatment of the major cathedrals in European countries.

Binns, J. *An Introduction to the Christian Orthodox Churches*. New York: Cambridge University Press, 2002. This recent introduction surveys the variety of manifestations of the Orthodox tradition throughout the world.

Bloesch, D. *The Church: Sacraments, Worship, Ministry, Mission.* Christian Foundations; Downers Grove, IL: InterVarsity Press, 2002. From the evangelical Protestant perspective, a statement of basic convictions concerning the several dimensions of the church.

Boff, Leonardo, and Boff, Clodovis. *Introducing Liberation Theology*. Maryknoll, NY: Orbis Books, 1987. Written by practitioners, this volume provides entry to the distinctive theological perspective originating in Europe but finding its most powerful expression in Latin America.

Brown, P. *The Rise of Western Christendom: Triumph and Diversity, A.D. 200–1000*. Cambridge, MA: Blackwells, 1996. A leading historian takes a fresh look at the remarkable development that was Christendom.

Brown, R. M. *The Ecumenical Revolution: An Interpretation of the Catholic-Protestant Dialogue*. Garden City, NJ: Doubleday, 1967. In the aftermath of the Second Vatican Council, an assessment of the achievements and possibilities for Christian unity.

Bynum, C. W. *Holy Feast and Holy Fast: The Religious Significance of Food for Medieval Women.* Berkeley: University of California Press, 1987. A leading feminist historian uncovers the complexities of women's experience in medieval Christianity.

————. *Jesus as Mother: Studies in the Spirituality of the High Middle Ages.* Berkeley: University of California Press, 1982. A thorough and inventive study of the surprising ways in which gender mattered and didn't matter in spiritual writings of medieval Christianity.

Carrington, P. *The Early Christian Church.* Vol. 2: *The Second Christian Century.* Cambridge: Cambridge University Press, 1957. This solidly researched and careful survey shows the developments and tensions in Christianity in its critical second century of existence.

Carroll, J. *Constantine's Sword: The Church and the Jews: A History.* Boston: Houghton Mifflin, 2001. Although excessive in some respects, this passionate account touches on the major issues concerning the long and tragic story of anti-Semitism in the Catholic tradition.

Chadwick, O. *The Reformation.* Baltimore: Penguin Books, 1964. Like the others in this series of Penguin histories, a reliable and readable survey of this period of Christian history in Europe, written by a notable historian.

Dillenberger, J., and Welch, C. *Protestant Christianity Interpreted through Its Development.* 2nd edition. New York: Macmillan, 1988. As its title suggests, this study seeks to define the multifaceted Protestant tradition in terms of historical changes and adaptations.

Dix, G. *The Shape of the Liturgy.* 2nd edition. New York: Seabury Press, 1982. This is the classic historical study of how Christian worship, above all in the Eucharist, developed from simple origins into its current configurations.

Dolan, J. P. *The American Catholic Experience: A History from Colonial Times to the Present.* Garden City, NJ: Doubleday, 1985. A substantial study of the distinctive way in which the Roman Catholic tradition developed from an immigrant to a truly American church.

Ellis, J. T. *American Catholicism*. Revised edition. Chicago: University of Chicago Press, 1969. Written earlier than Dolan (see above) by the dean of American Roman Catholic historians, a standard treatment of the American version of Catholicism.

Eusebius of Caesarea. *Life of Constantine*. Translation and commentary by A. Cameron and S. G. Hall. Oxford: Clarendon Press, 1999. The biography by the 4th-century Christian historian that portrays the emperor as a hero of the faith, a symbolic expression of "Constantinianism."

Ferm, D. W. *Third World Liberation Theologies: An Introductory Survey*. Maryknoll, NY: Orbis Books, 1986. This book provides the names and works by the many theologians who have sought to align Christianity more with the poor than the powerful.

Forrell, G. W. (ed.). *Christian Social Teachings: A Reader in Christian Social Ethics from the Bible to the Present*. Minneapolis: Augsburg Publishing, 1966. A useful compendium of primary source materials illustrating the spectrum of positions taken by Christians on social issues.

Fox, R. L. *Pagans and Christians*. San Francisco: HarperSanFrancisco, 1986. A popular but responsible account of Christianity's steady progression into Greco-Roman culture between 30 and 600 A.D.

Frederick J. L. *Faith among Faiths: Christian Theology and Non-Christian Religions*. New York: Paulist Press, 1999. A positive treatment of the way Christian theologians are seeking to respond to the implications of the experience of global pluralism for Christian self-understanding.

Frend, W. H. C. *Martyrdom and Persecution in the Early Church*. A careful and influential study of the hard circumstances in which Christianity made its way in the world over the first three centuries.

Gilson, E. *The History of Christian Philosophy in the Middle Ages*. London: Sheed and Ward, 1955. Written by a fine historian who was also deeply appreciative of Scholastic philosophy, this survey discusses the main figures and variations in that powerful medieval synthesis of Christianity and Aristotle.

Grant, R. M., and Tracy, D. *A Short History of the Interpretation of the Bible*. 2nd revised and enlarged edition. Philadelphia: Fortress Press, 1984. An accessible introduction to the major moments in the complex history of biblical interpretation within Christianity.

Haddad, Y. Y., and Esposito, J. L. *Daughters of Abraham: Feminist Thought in Judaism, Christianity and Islam*. A collection of essays that surveys the efforts of feminist theologians to rethink patriarchal traditions within the three world religions of the West.

Hamilton, M. P. (ed.). *The Charismatic Movement*. Grand Rapids, MI: Eerdmans, 1975. A collection of essays concentrating on the ecumenical phenomenon of Pentecostalism during the 1960s and 1970s.

Hays, R. B. *The Moral Vision of the New Testament: Community, Cross, New Creation: A Contemporary Introduction to New Testament Ethics*. San Francisco: HarperSanFrancisco, 1996. A constructive effort to make the New Testament pertinent to contemporary ethics, notable for its close reading of the New Testament and its engagement with contemporary Christian ethicists.

Hollenweger, W. J. *The Pentecostals*. Minneapolis: Augsburg Publishing, 1972. A study of those Christians for whom the manifest gifts of the Holy Spirit—especially speaking in tongues—is of first importance.

Johnson, L. T. *Religious Experience in Earliest Christianity: A Missing Dimension in New Testament Studies*. Minneapolis: Fortress Press, 1998. A study of earliest Christianity that emphasizes its specifically religious dimension. See also the Teaching Company course *Earliest Christianity: Experience of the Divine*.

————. *The Creed: What Christians Believe and Why It Matters*. New York: Doubleday, 2003. An effort to show that the 4th- century Nicene Creed provides a contemporary guide to Scripture, as well as Christian practices.

————. *The Writings of the New Testament: An Interpretation*. 2nd revised edition. Minneapolis: Fortress Press, 1998. This introduction deals with the anthropological, historical, literary, and religious dimensions of the classic Christian texts.

Johnson, P. *A History of Christianity*. New York: Athenaeum, 1976. A sometimes idiosyncratic but lively and informed popular history, with an unusual selection of heroes and villains.

Jungmann, J. A. *The Mass: An Historical, Theological, and Pastoral Survey*. Translated by E. Fernandez, edited by M. E. Evans. Collegeville, MN: Liturgical Press, 1975. The central liturgy of the Roman Catholic tradition, surveyed by a leading historian of the Eucharist.

Kelly, J. N. D. *Early Christian Creeds*. London: Longmans, 1960. A companion to his *Early Christian Doctrines*, this book traces, with Kelly's usual finesse and learning, the development of statements of belief in earliest Christianity.

————. *Early Christian Doctrines*. Revised edition. San Francisco: Harper and Row, 1960. A straightforward and well-informed explanation of how and why critical Christian teachings developed over the first four centuries.

Kinnamon, M., and Cope, B. E. *The Ecumenical Movement: An Anthology of Key Texts and Voices*. Grand Rapids: Eerdmans, 1997. A helpful collection of primary texts that illustrate the movement toward Christian unity in the 20th century.

Knox, R. A. *Enthusiasm: A Chapter in the History of Religion*. A classic study of movements within Christianity that emphasized the experience of the Holy Spirit, especially those that led to conflict and division.

Kugel, J. L., and Greer, R.A. *Early Biblical Interpretation*. Library of Early Christianity; Philadelphia: Westminster Press, 1986. A study valuable especially for showing how early Christian and Jewish interpretations of the Bible were both similar and dissimilar.

Kung, H., and Moltmann, J.(eds.). *Christianity and World Religions*. Concilium; Edinburgh: T & T Clark, 1986. A collection of essays by Christian theologians seeking a positive relationship with other world religions, valuable because of its attention to specific world religions.

Lake, K. (ed.). *The Apostolic Fathers*. The Loeb Classical Library; Cambridge: Harvard University Press, 1915. An accessible edition in Greek and English of the basic Christian texts of the late 1st and early 2nd centuries.

Layton, B. (ed.). *The Gnostic Scriptures*. Garden City, NJ: Doubleday, 1987. A collection of the most important writings produced by the Gnostic movement, with helpful introductions and notes.

Lea, H. C. *The Inquisition of the Middle Ages: Its Organization and Operation*. New York: Harper and Row, 1963. A straightforward and informative treatment of the mechanisms for suppressing difference by the medieval church.

LeClerq, Jean. *The Love of Learning and the Desire for God: A Study of Monastic Culture*. 2nd revised edition, translated by C. Misrahi. New York: Fordham University Press, 1974. A classic appreciation of the distinctive combination of piety and scholarship that pervaded monasteries before the rise of the medieval university.

Leith, J. H. (ed.). *Creeds of the Churches: A Reader in Christian Doctrine from the Bible to the Present*. Atlanta: John Knox Press, 1982. Makes available in English translation, with helpful commentary, the major statements of belief produced by Christian communities.

Lietzmann, H. *Mass and Lord's Supper: A Study in the History of the Liturgy*. Translated by D. H. G. Reave, with introduction and further inquiry by R. D.

Richardson. Leiden: E.J. Brill, 1979. A rich resource for the sources of the Christian liturgy and a classic example of historical analysis into tradition.

Macquarrie, J. *A Guide to the Sacraments*. New York: Continuum, 1997. A simple, yet substantial introduction by a major theologian to the meaning of the sacraments within Christianity.

Marsden, G. *Fundamentalism and American Culture: The Shaping of Twentieth-Century Evangelicalism, 1870–1925*. New York: Oxford University Press, 1980. An important and influential study of fundamentalism as a response to modernity.

Marty, M. E. *Protestantism*. New York: Holt, Rinehart and Winston, 1972. Like the others in this series, an accessible survey of this complex version of Christianity, written with authority and grace.

————. *Righteous Empire: The Protestant Experience in America*. New York: Dial Press, 1970. A major statement by one of the most influential church historians and public theologians in America.

McBrien, R. P. *Catholicism*. 2 vols. Minneapolis: Winston Press, 1980. A major statement on Roman Catholicism reflecting the tensions in that tradition 15 years after the conclusion of the Second Vatican Council.

McGinn, B. *The Presence of God: A History of Western Mysticism*. 3 vols. New York: Crossroad, 2000. A major study of the mystics in the Western church in their historical context.

McKenzie, J. L. *The Roman Catholic Church*. New York: Holt, Rinehart and Winston, 1969. Written within a few years of the Second Vatican Council, an effort to describe the basic lineaments of Catholicism by an author with the gift of simplicity.

Meeks, W. A. *The First Urban Christians: The Social World of the Apostle Paul*. New Haven: Yale University Press, 1983. A deservedly influential study of earliest Christianity using the perspectives of the social sciences.

————. *The Origins of Christian Morality: The First Two Centuries*. New Haven: Yale University Press, 1993. A study that shows the relationship between forming communities and forming moral character and the multiple ways that happened in the first two Christian centuries.

Meyendorff, J. *The Orthodox Church: Its Past and Its Role in the World Today*. 3rd revised edition. Crestwood, NY: St. Vladimir's Seminary Press, 1981. A statement by a major figure in American Orthodoxy that is both descriptive and normative.

Murray, P. *The Oxford Companion to Christian Art and Architecture*. New York: Oxford University Press, 1996. A necessarily partial guide to the major works and artists in this complex and rich history.

Neill, S. *A History of Christian Missions*. 2nd revised edition by O. Chadwick. New York: Penguin, 1986. A crisp treatment of a major subject by a leading expert; revised by an equally fine scholar.

Niebuhr, H. R. *Christ and Culture*. New York: Harper and Row, 1951. A seminal work that proposes a typology of responses within Christianity to the larger culture; constantly corrected by others in detail, but perennially illuminating.

O'Donovan, O., and O'Donovan, J. L. *From Irenaeus to Grotius: A Sourcebook in Christian Political Thought*. Grand Rapids: Eerdmans, 1999. A valuable collection of primary texts representing the wide spectrum of views in the history of Christianity on the political order and religion's relation to it.

Parker, T. *Christianity and the State in the Light of History*. London: A&C Black, 1955. A short survey of Christianity's different postures toward the political order over its history in the West.

Pelikan, J. *The Excellent Empire: The Fall of Rome and the Triumph of the Church*. San Francisco: HarperSanFrancisco, 1987. A brilliant revisiting of

Bibliography

Gibbon, looking again at the role of Constantine and Theodosius in shaping the Christian empire.

———. *Jesus through the Centuries: His Place in the History of Culture.* New York: Perennial Library, 1987. A groundbreaking study of the ways in which Jesus has shaped culture and, in turn, been shaped by culture.

———. *Mary through the Centuries: Her Place in the History of Culture.* New Haven: Yale University Press, 1996. Pelikan does for the mother of Jesus what he did for her son; that is, shows how she figured in the culture of Christendom.

———. *The Illustrated Jesus through the Centuries.* New Haven: Yale University Press, 1997. The companion volume to *Jesus through the Centuries* (see above), providing a rich set of pictures and icons.

Quasten, J. *Patrology.* 4 vols. Westminster, MD: Christian Classics, 1983. An authoritative handbook, providing full bibliographical information on all the Christian literature of the first five centuries.

Rauschenbusch, W. *A Theology of the Social Gospel.* Nashville, TN: Abingdon Press, 1945. A classic exposition of the understanding of Christianity in terms of a liberal commitment to social betterment.

Runciman, S. *A History of the Crusades.* 3 vols. New York: Harper and Row, 1964. A comprehensive and detailed examination of the military expeditions launched by Christians in the West to conquer the Holy Lands controlled by Muslims.

Sandeen, E. *The Roots of Fundamentalism: British and American Millenarianism, 1800–1930.* Chicago: University of Chicago Press, 1970. A treatment of evangelical Protestantism that emphasizes its roots in eschatology rather than in its rejection of modernity (see Marsden).

Schmemann, A. *For the Life of the World: Sacraments and Orthodoxy.* 2nd revised and expanded edition. Crestwood, NY: St. Vladimir's Seminary

Press, 1988. A study of Orthodoxy, with particular attention to the centrality of worship and the sacraments in this tradition.

———. *The Historical Road of Eastern Orthodoxy*. Translated by L. W. Kesich. New York: Holt, Rinehart and Winston, 1963. Like the other volumes in this introductory series (see Marty and McKenzie), an attractive introduction to the tradition by one of its major spokespersons.

Senn, F. C. (ed.). *Protestant Spiritual Traditions*. New York: Paulist Press, 1986. A representative sample of the spiritual riches and resources within a tradition that is sometimes thought to be lacking in them.

Shaw, M. *The Kingdom of God in Africa: A Short History of African Christianity*. Grand Rapids: Baker Books, 1996. A necessarily broad view of a complex subject, this volume provides some background to the explosion of Christianity in that continent.

Smalley, B. *The Study of the Bible in the Middle Ages*. Notre Dame: University of Notre Dame Press, 1964. An important study that shows how lively medieval study of the Bible was and how lively was the exchange between Jewish and Christian teachers in that era.

Southern, R. W. *Western Society and the Church in the Middle Ages*. New York: Penguin Books, 1970. As with other books in the Penguin series, a readable introduction to a complex period in the history of Christianity by a leading scholar.

Sunquist, S. W. (ed.). *A Dictionary of Asian Christianity*. Grand Rapids: Eerdmans, 2001. Christianity is finding increased success among Asian populations, and this dictionary provides some helpful guidance to places, people, and phenomena.

Sweeney, L. *Christian Philosophy: Greek, Medieval, Contemporary Reflections*. New York: Peter Lang, 1997. A study that examines the different forms of engagement between Christianity and philosophy at different periods.

Thompson, B. *Liturgies of the Western Church.* Philadelphia: Fortress Press, 1961. A useful collection of primary sources in translation of liturgies used in the Roman Catholic and Protestant traditions.

Verhey, A. *Remembering Jesus: Christian Community, Scripture, and the Moral Life.* Grand Rapids: Eerdmans, 2002. A major study of the ways in which Christian communities can engage the Bible in thinking about such moral issues as health, the economy, sexuality, and politics.

Vidler, A. R. *The Church in an Age of Revolution: 1789 to the Present Day.* Baltimore: Penguin Books, 1961. Another in the series of excellent Penguin histories, this one showing the impact of new political forces in Europe and the various strategies of response developed in different Christian bodies.

Wagner, W. H. *After the Apostles: Christianity in the Second Century.* Minneapolis: Fortress Press, 1994. An excellent short study that shows how Christianity faced its decisive moment of self-definition in response to powerful alternative visions.

Ware, T. *The Orthodox Church.* New York: Penguin Books, 1963. A short introduction to the tradition that puts particular emphasis on the centrality of worship.

Weaver, M. J. *Introduction to Christianity.* 3rd edition, with D. Bakke and J. Bivins . Belmont, CA: Wadsworth Press, 1998. A thorough yet readable introduction at the college level that is wonderfully attuned to contemporary issues without losing sight of the weight of tradition.

————. *New Catholic Women: A Contemporary Challenge to Traditional Religious Authority.* Bloomington: Indiana University Press, 1995. An important statement of feminism in Catholicism based on sound historical research.

Williams, M. A. *Rethinking Gnosticism: An Argument for the Dismantling of a Dubious Category.* Princeton: Princeton University Press, 1996. Despite its daunting title, a readable and learned reexamination of our actual knowledge of this early Christian phenomenon.